THE PRIDE

THE PRIDE

A Family of Killers Fighting to Survive

MICHAEL BRIGHT

BOOKS

First published in Great Britain in 2010 by
JR Books, 10 Greenland Street, London NW1 0ND
www.jrbooks.com

A catalogue record for this book is available from the British Library.

ISBN 978-1-906779-77-1

1 3 5 7 9 10 8 6 4 2

Printed and bound by MPG Books, Bodmin, Cornwall.

To Giannina and Jonathan

Contents

CHAPTER ONE

– Masa's Tale –

A bolt of lightning rent the air with such a thunderous roar, it shook the very Earth itself. Every living thing cowered in the face of such devastating power . . . all except a young lioness: she had other things on her mind. Her large belly betrayed her secret: it was nearly time for her to give birth and she had to find shelter soon or the newly born cubs would not survive the deluge. She had been hiding in the dense vegetation close to the river, a favoured birthing site for lionesses of the resident pride, but the rains had swollen its waters and the swamp would soon be completely under water. She struggled to gain a foothold, slipped and her rear legs sank into the liquid mud. Slowly, using her powerful forelimbs and claws, she hauled herself on to a clump of reeds that had been flattened by elephants. They were long gone, heading out to fight for the right to mate and the promise of lush, green grass on the open plains, but she was here and needed to be somewhere else, and fast.

She paused for a moment's rest, and then tackled the steep and rocky slope that would lead her to a labyrinth of crevices and shallow caves, a welcome refuge from the storm. She clambered increasingly higher up the slope. It became almost vertical, so she kept slipping and sliding, a few paces forward and seemingly a lot more back. She was on the crater side of a gigantic, extinct volcano that blew its top and collapsed in on itself about three millions years ago.

The rain was lashing down and the wind carried great walls of spray. As rain turned to hail, the lioness tried to hide behind the slender trunk of small yellow-barked acacia that was bent over like a bow. The tiny hailstones stripped leaves from the tree and stung her face. Masa – for that was the name given her by watching scientists – had scaled part way up the crater slope, a great circular wall over 600 metres high that enclosed a vast and ancient caldera containing 260 square kilometres of open grassland and scattered woodlands – a microcosm of the African savannah. Thousands of large animals resided there, mostly herbivores like wildebeest and zebra, but including the highest density of large mammalian predators in Africa.

On reaching the rocks, Masa hesitated. She was one of those predators, but this was leopard country. The smaller cat was unlikely to attack a full-grown lioness, but a mother leopard defending cubs could inflict serious wounds if disturbed, and the lioness could ill afford to be compromised at a time like this. She stepped carefully, sniffing suspiciously at every entrance for signs of danger.

With the rain still falling and bedraggled and cold from her rain-sodden fur, she settled on a cleft in the rocks protected by a large, rocky overhang. It was a good hideaway and a convenient lookout, commanding a clear view over the surrounding slopes and the crater floor. Little would go unnoticed; at least, when the storm had passed, for visibility on this day was almost nothing. She shook the water from her coat and flopped on to the ground. Sitting like a miniature sphinx, her regal head turned slowly first left and then right as her stark yellow eyes surveyed her temporary home. She blinked . . . slowly, in that way lions tend to do, suggestive of an animal at ease with the world.

Masa was in her prime, a magnificent lioness with a pale buff pelage grading to almost white on her belly. The faint imprint of her baby spots could still be seen on her flanks and down her muscular legs, and the tuft of hair at the tip of her tail was jet black. She stood about a metre high at the shoulder, and weighed a good 150 kilos, large for an East African lioness. When she yawned, fearsome canine teeth, eight centimetres long betrayed her role in the scheme of things. She was one of Africa's supreme predators, but soon she would be a mother. Her contractions were increasing, but she would be waiting for darkness before giving birth.

By evening, the rain had stopped and a thick mist cloaked the blue-green slopes. Humidity was high. A rainbow pointed to what looked like crocks of gold as a shaft of golden sunlight illuminated the beige backs of Thomson's gazelles that had come down for their evening drink at the river delta feeding into the crater lake. Nearby, a group of black rhino wallowed in the pale grey mud, looking to all the world like giant, four-legged ghosts in the fading light. A family party of giraffes, spooked by something hiding in a thicket, lolloped away into the distance, sparking a line of wildebeest to break into a gallop. A group of zebra scratched their pyjama-striped hides against large, dark boulders scattered amongst tall, brown grass and looked on disdainfully.

The last rays of the sun lit the crater rim, while the faint orb of the moon peaked out from behind billowing clouds that had gathered over the highlands nearby. A pair of crowned cranes honked loudly, and the deep roar of lions and the whooping calls of hyenas revealed that the larger predators were beginning to gather for their heinous activities in the night . . . and then the contractions began again. It was nearly time.

Like Masa, all lioness mothers retire to a safe place to give birth, but when their cubs are big and fit enough to travel, they return to their pride where they bring up their offspring in the company of others. Many of a pride's lionesses conceive and give birth at roughly the same time so each can help the other to rear their cubs. Masa, however, had no pride. She was a loner, but not by choice. Her story was a tragic tale.

Masa was brought up with the Lake Pride, a formidable band of lions who dominated the shores of a large soda lake on the floor of the crater. As a young lioness she was always in trouble, getting up to all kinds of mischief, like chasing birds and climbing trees, but most of the other lionesses tolerated her tomfoolery, for when the time came for the chase, she was always at the front, ready to throw herself, quite literally, at the prey. She learned well from her own mother and the other females in the pride to become a highly accomplished huntress.

There was, however, one detractor – Hasimu, a middle-aged lioness who always took a back seat at hunts but was always first at the table after the kill, and she seemed to have it in for Masa. She obstructed her at every opportunity and was quick to take a swipe at her during the free-for-all that inevitably accompanied feeding time. Masa avoided her if at all possible, preferring the company of the other females in the pride.

These little niggles aside, the Lake Pride, however, went from strength to strength, increasing in numbers, seizing territory from neighbouring prides, and taking the lion's share of available food. It was invincible; that is, until the great rains came. Following a period of prolonged drought, during which the pride thrived by scavenging mainly on the dead and dying, there were two long years of almost continuous rain, the likes of which had never been seen before; and with the rain came pestilence.

A small insect – the stable fly – was to blame. From the month of May in the second rain-soaked year, the crater became a hell on Earth. The fly was a close relative of the common housefly, but this species was much more sinister – it bit and drew blood like the dreaded tsetse fly. Equipped with tiny teeth on its tongue-like labium, it pierced the skin of its hosts and sucked their blood. Female flies had to be gorged before they produced eggs, and there was blood aplenty. Every mammal in the area, large or small, suffered greatly. A bloodsucking swarm could bleed an animal to death within a few days, and lions took the full brunt.

Stable fly numbers increased to such an extent they soon reached plague proportions. The flies came in clouds and the lions were forced to seek refuge from them in trees and down hyena burrows, but wherever they went they could not avoid being attacked. Many of Masa's pride were covered in festering sores and were unhealthily thin. They became so ill that they were unable to hunt, and one by one they died. A previously healthy population of seventy lions in five prides was reduced to just eight hardy survivors – seven females and a male. Masa was one of those who survived, but almost all of the rest of her pride were gone. Ironically, the only other lioness to make it was the thorn in her flesh – Hasimu – and so, reluctantly, Masa teamed up with her former rival in order that they might eat. With a welcome dry season breaking up the almost continuous wet, the surviving lionesses could go stalking again. As it happened, Masa did most of the hunting and Hasimu most of the eating. Hasimu must have been the laziest lioness in Africa, and she was also one of the luckiest.

Early one morning, three or four months after the start of the dry, there was the unmistakable roar of a lion, in fact, two lions. Masa and Hasimu stopped in their tracks. It was a sound they had not heard for some time, and it was coming from the rim of the crater, at the top of a track that was kept clear of vegetation by bull elephants who visited the crater to rest and re-charge their batteries between bouts of fighting, courtship and mating. Both the lionesses made for cover. They looked back up the steep slope and waited. The roars were getting louder. Whoever was making them was heading down the path and into the crater.

It was then that they saw the two strangers, two magnificent lions very much in their prime. They strutted rather than walked down the slope. Following their own barrage of roars there had been none in return, so the two males surmised that there were no rivals to ruin their ambitions. They were full of confidence and showed it. With all the old kings dead, young pretenders to the crater throne were beginning to appear, and they were looking for females to set up their own prides. Previously, the resident males were so strong, few if any lions from the neighbouring plains were able to take over the crater prides. It was a closed shop, but now things were different.

The two males were not related. When they had reached the age of three years, each had been ejected from his natal pride, and now they were both prospecting for a pride of their own. While nomads, they had formed a coalition. Alone they would have had difficulty taking over any pride, but working together they were a force to be reckoned with.

They came closer to the place where the two lionesses were hiding. Masa and Hasimu peered out from behind the foliage. They could see the older male had dark, tan fur and a full, ginger mane. His younger companion was darker, with a black mane. Hasimu ran out and lay prostrate on the ground in front of the two lions, startling them momentarily. They quickly regained their composure and sniffed at the lioness. Masa was more reticent and remained hidden. The lions sniffed the air. They knew she was there but did nothing to scare her away.

Hasimu, meanwhile, continued to ingratiate herself with the new arrivals, and the three of them swaggered down the track and into the crater. Masa followed at a discrete distance, and watched as other lionesses appeared from the undergrowth. The boys were gathering a harem, and without even trying. Lions and lionesses could survive well enough alone, living on small prey that was not shared with others, but when it came to rearing cubs it was better to be in a group, to have the pride as protection, and these lionesses were forming a pride, albeit a highly unusual pride of mostly unrelated females. There were only a few examples on record of unrelated females joining together, but these were extraordinary times and it called for extraordinary measures in order for them to thrive.

Eventually, the procession reached the lake and had entered the old territory of the Lake Pride, where the two lions flopped down below a large tree. Hasimu was already on head-rubbing terms with the ginger-maned male, so she lay down beside him. The others gathered around in an untidy group. It was getting on for midday and the sun was high in the sky and the temperature rising.

Masa, who had still not joined the group, saw that the moment was right. She emerged from the undergrowth and walked towards the two males. The lion with the black mane rose, walked towards her and sniffed. She opened her mouth, bared her canines and snarled a little . . . but not too much. He roared directly at her. The sound was so intense, it went through her entire body. Then he called a truce and lay down again. Masa was just about to do the same when Hasimu charged her, biting and scratching at her face. Masa retreated.

The two males, somewhat taken aback, leapt to their feet, but did not intervene. Hasimu continued her attack, driving Masa back up the track. When two of the other lioness got up and started heading her way, she ran.

And so it was that Masa was excluded from the pride. Hasimu saw to that. Masa followed them for days on end, but every time she made contact, Hasimu blocked her at every move. She would have to fend for herself, but it was not easy hunting alone in an area dominated by the new pride. And it was not just lions that she had to watch. There were other creatures here that could also make her life a misery.

One day, Masa had brought down a wildebeest calf but she could not take advantage of her kill. She was looking intently in the direction of several hyenas that were lolloping towards her. They had picked up the scent of the carcass and were closing in. At first, Masa snarled at them, and rushed them, but their whoops and cackles attracted even more of the clan. Vultures were also arriving, and even a jackal. But she lunged at them once too often and within seconds she had been brushed aside and they were tearing apart the body. All Masa could do was to watch from a safe distance and wait for them to finish. Such was the appetite of hyenas, however, there was unlikely to be anything left.

Masa made a snap decision. She rushed them. They could easily overcome a lone lioness, but with surprise on her side they scattered and left the carcass unguarded. She grabbed it and made for a thicket, but she was not quick enough. The hyenas regrouped and came back at her. She made a play at defending her kill but had to give in. They had superior numbers. She dropped it and ran for cover. She would not try a second time.

At the peak of the dry season, prey was especially wary, and Masa had to pass through the territories of several newly established prides to find a victim she could bring down alone. It was a clear moonlit night, and a myopic zebra was standing alone, seemingly unaware that she was there. Masa began to stalk. She moved forward when the zebra lowered its head to graze and froze when it looked up. She inched towards it, and it was not until she charged from only a couple of metres away that the animal reacted. It was far too late. Masa had it by the throat and it was dead in minutes. She had succeeded in bringing down a substantial beast. This should have kept her going for several days, but it was not to be.

She quickly opened the body cavity and ripped out the entrails, gorging quickly on the soft parts before slicing into the meat. But she spotted movement out of the corner of her eye. She looked up and there, not more than a few metres away, were two hyenas. They fussed about nervously while Masa stood over her carcass, but they dare not approach. Masa returned to her meal, but one of her visitors started to whoop. Within a few minutes, the two hyenas had grown to ten, and then 20, but it was not these animals she feared, it was what else the disturbance might attract.

Out of the darkness, two male lions appeared. It was the new pride male and his older companion. Masa fled to a nearby thicket as they tore into the hyenas, scattering them in all directions. The rest of the pride, with Hasimu amongst them, was right behind. They gathered around the carcass, waiting for the two lions to finish. They had scavenged Masa's hard-earned kill, and all she could do was hide in the scrub until the moment came when she could slink away.

The following morning was hot nearly from daybreak. Dust devils whipped across the dried grassland and, as Masa wandered down to the lake, she came across the putrid remains of a dead baby hippo. It was besieged by vultures and jackals, but she barged her way in to find only skin and bones were left. She chewed on what she could before the first hyenas arrived, and then left before any trouble started. The hyenas, in turn, demolished what the other scavengers could not eat, so barely a stain was left on the ground.

It was then that she ran into someone who would change her life for ever. She had clambered up the crater slope to avoid Hasimu and the pride, when there on the path ahead was a large male lion. He was very different from the other two males in that his fur was a pale buff and his full, flowing mane was blond. Masa could not avoid him, so instead she stopped and waited. Both lion and lioness stared at each other. He sniffed the air, then shifted so that his body was sideways to her. He cut a fine figure, although he was a little past his prime.

He had once lived in the crater, brought up here as a cub, just as Masa had been. But when he came of age, he and his brother were chased away by the resident males and not allowed to return. They roamed the plains and eventually took over a group of lionesses, but not that long ago nomads killed his brother and he lost possession of their pride. He had been wandering as a solitary nomad, using his strength and his wits to survive alone. And now, he had returned home. With the old regime gone, he was able to enter the crater and had not yet encountered any of the newly established prides.

He walked up to Masa. Sniffed some more. Tested the air. She stood remarkably still, waiting for the inevitable attack. Minutes seemed like hours, and then he did nothing. He stopped, stared into the distance, and just walked away. She watched him go, but then he stopped, turned back to look at her, before continuing down the track. She followed.

Masa and her blond male stayed together for several months – a kind of mini-pride, but they were always careful to remain on the periphery of pride territories and to avoid any confrontations. She was the expert huntress, he the strong protector. It was a winning formula. Occasionally they would bump into pride lionesses, but they usually escaped without a fight; like the time they had brought down a wildebeest on the edge of the marsh near the lake, right in the resident pride's territory. They ate quickly and nervously, looking up every few minutes to check for danger. A single hyena was first to find them. It whooped loudly and before long a dozen had joined the two lions at the carcass – lions on one side, hyenas on the other, each of them wolfing down food as fast as they could.

Suddenly the hyenas dispersed, and over a rise came the dark-maned lion. Masa and her partner fled, leaving the carcass behind, and not before time. The rest of the pride appeared, but they had been beaten to the food. The male appropriated the kill. The females got nothing. Instead, they roared loudly in the direction that Masa had disappeared.

When the wet season arrived, however, the two companions ate well. For hors d'oeuvre there were termites. As the rains arrived, billions upon billions of winged termites, each with its fat, juicy abdomen, spilled from termite mounds for their nuptial flight. It was a gastronomic orgy with bateleur eagles and storks swooping in from the sky, along with the more familiar insect-eaters – drongos, shrikes, rollers and swallows. Frogs and marsh mongooses emerged from the swamp to grab what they could, and even the lions snacked on the fluttering insects when they hit the ground.

For main course, they had a range of meats. Gradually, the marsh area flooded, but instead of moving to higher ground, like the rest of the lion community, they remained behind, catching waterbuck and warthog. Waterbuck were relatively easy to bring down, at least the males were. Instead of running, they would stand and fight so Masa kept them busy at the front end while the blond male leapt on them from the rear. It worked every time. And there were other benefits. Running through water and over waterlogged ground meant that Masa's leg and chest muscles were thickening. She was becoming bigger and stronger and more than a match for any of the pride females. She was also developing her hunting skills even more. She would not sit back and watch others do all the work, as Hasimu had done, but did it all herself or together with her hunting partner.

But they could never have a place of their own, no matter how strong they were. With fewer than three lionesses and at least two lions, a pride would be pressed to hold down a territory in the crater, so Masa would always be a refugee, avoiding spats with residents, living a life always on the edge; although there were a few occasions when the males of the resident pride relented.

Masa and her partner where lying in a clearing when the two pride males suddenly appeared. For some unknown reason, they did not attack but lay down not more than 100 metres away. Masa stood and walked deliberately towards the dark-maned male and rubbed heads. He pulled back his lips, exposing his teeth but made no sound. She walked away, without looking back. Her companion rose slowly and followed. The pride males remained where they were and did not attack.

There were humorous moments too. They lay down to rest by an old rotting tree trunk and found that they were not alone. Besides a red-headed woodpecker that was hammering for grubs and a party of weaverbirds that were squabbling more than they were foraging, it was also home to a gang of banded mongooses. One by one they popped out and lined up like spectators at a freak show, unsure what to do about the predators on their doorstep. They began to chatter noisily, by which point the lioness had had enough and leaped up. The mongooses scattered, but Masa was so incensed she chased one through the forest – over and under fallen branches, across clearings and around termite mounds. Eventually, the mongoose dived for cover and disappeared down a burrow, leaving Masa to vent her frustration on a spindly bush.

And there were surprises, like the bull elephant they encountered early one morning. It was a chilly start to the day. Mist filled the crater, and cold air flowed down the slopes. It would still be another hour before the sun peaked over the crater rim, so the two lions were active before the temperature rose. They were out hunting, but the combination of mist and dim light meant that they were almost on top of prey before they saw them, removing any chance of a surprise attack. It also meant they walked straight into the elephant. He had been gouging out rock at a known elephant mineral lick, and was heading back down into the bowl of the crater.

Now, the bulls in the crater are not especially aggressive – their worst offence was to prune all the trees – but this one was clearly out of sorts. His ears flapped wildly as he walked along the well-worn path, and when confronted suddenly with two lions, he went berserk, throwing his head about, thrashing at the undergrowth with his trunk and trumpeting loudly. Masa froze. She had never seen an elephant behaving this way before. This was one mean beast, big and powerful, and intelligent too.

Her partner bumped her and they both ran. They hid behind a croton bush, but they could hear that the elephant was coming towards them. They ran again, this time stopping behind a small fig tree, and waited. The elephant was destroying something, but they could not see. Then, it came on again. They fled to a marshy area and looked back. Through a gap in the mist they could see the elephant pushing over the fig tree behind which they had been hiding. It was following their scent and systematically destroying every place they had been. It was a killer, and it was still coming their way.

They ran again, deeper into the swamp, but the elephant stopped at the edge of the marshy ground. He had lost the scent. Instead, he walked back and forth, thrashing the vegetation and trumpeting continuously. Masa and her companion trotted on. They were safe. As the sun chased the mist away, they could still hear him in the distance, but now it was time to find food. Pricking their ears, they not only heard the elephant, but also distant hyenas.

Travelling about a kilometre, they found the group. They had killed a wildebeest, but there were only a few. Masa and her male rushed them and took over the carcass, but they were not the only ones to take a look. Hasimu and two lionesses from the pride were approaching. Masa's companion ignored them and continued to eat. Masa, however, was ready to attack. She ran at Hasimu, who snarled and swiped the air with her forepaw, but Masa was quick. She grabbed her rival's neck, drawing blood. Hasimu rolled over, but Masa was on her, swiped at her head and knocked her down again, and again, and again. There was no stopping her. She tore into Hasimu, clawing and biting. The older lioness reeled from the blows, and deep gashes appeared on her face and side. She rolled on to her back in a submissive posture, but Masa was unrelenting. She grabbed her by the throat and did not let go. The older lioness was suffocating, as if she were prey. But, as the life was slowly draining from her body, the pride males suddenly appeared.

Masa saw them coming. She let go of Hasimu and ran for cover. Her companion, however, was slow to his feet. The pride males were on him in seconds, and the fight was to the death. The blond male put up a brave defence, but he had little chance against the younger lions. They left him on the ground. He was barely alive when Masa returned. She licked his head and his wounds, but it was all to no avail. He died right there and then. She lay down beside is lifeless body.

From now on Masa had not only to hunt alone again but also avoid the lion prides, and they were getting increasingly more powerful, each pride taking over a territory containing a body of water, to the exclusion of other lions. It was no easy task weaving a life in between. She had to make do with whatever the land could provide, and on one memorable occasion it was warthog. She stalked the family, a mother and her entourage of piglets, for several minutes, just waiting for the opportunity to pounce. The moment came. She raced out from behind a bush, the family ran, but not before she grabbed a piglet and made off. This mother, though, was not to be trifled with. She raced after Masa, and the lioness barely kept ahead of her. Warthogs are remarkably fast, even on their stumpy legs. Masa reached a fallen tree but just as she was about to leap on to the trunk, the warthog smashed into her side, almost knocking her off balance. She struggled to gain her footing and leaped clear, the piglet still in her mouth. Once on the log she was out of reach, and so she simply waited until the mother left. Her prey was little more than a snack, but at least it was food.

Masa, though, had been slow to avoid the mother warthog. It was not like her at all. She was also agitated of late, and she felt prickly as the temperature soared at midday. She was also showing signs of a paunch, which was clearly not through overeating and lack of exercise. No, the thickened skin around her teats gave it way. Masa was pregnant.

The contractions were coming thick and fast. Masa was lying on a natural bed of dead leaves that had blown into the cave and, as she pushed hard, the first baby began to appear. It was coming back legs first and, as it emerged, tiny claws on its rear feet cut the foetal sac. Masa bit the umbilical cord, ate the afterbirth and licked her firstborn clean of dirt, mucous and the remains of the foetal sac. This was Moja, a female. She was born with her eyes closed, deaf and utterly defenceless. An hour passed before there were more contractions, and second to arrive was Mbili, a male cub. After another hour Masa stood, crouched and pushed out Tatu, the third cub, another male. He hung momentarily in mid-air, but when his back claws cut the sac he was lowered gently to the ground. Just over an hour later Masa lay down again and a fourth cub Nne, another female, was eased out of its warm, snug womb and into a cold, harsh world. Four cubs, almost identical except that each already showed its own pattern of whisker spots on either side of its muzzle, a feature that would remain from cradle to grave and which was as unique to each of those lion cubs as a human fingerprint.

Masa rested, her four newly born cubs nestling into the thick fur on her belly. Instinctively they reached to drink, and they suckled contentedly for all of ten minutes. It was thirsty work being born!

CHAPTER TWO

– Cubs In Peril –

Masa kept her cubs at the cave for nearly a month. Their eyes opened when they were four days old, revealing not the stark yellow eyes of their mother. They would change when they were older, but for now they were surprisingly blue. All the cubs also had thick woolly fur. Moja and Nne, the two female cubs, and Tatu, the younger male, had tan coats, like their mother, but Mbili was altogether different. Already his fur was very pale, almost white, like his father, which might be attractive to the human eye but could be a distinct disadvantage on the dry, beige-coloured or the green, rain-soaked savannah. For now, however, he was safe in the den, protected by an attentive mother.

As he was suckled, Mbili placed his paw on his mother's stomach, closed his eyes and drank milk for what must have been ten minutes at least. When he had finished he placed his head on his mother's back and looked out contentedly across the grassland. What a big world it was, this crater, a world for adventures. A comforting lick across the top of his head, brought him out of his daydream. He rubbed his mother's chin, cuffed her cheeks and played with her tail, before lying on his back with his paws in the air, a very contented lion cub.

Mother left them in the den for short periods to go hunting and refresh her milk supply. At first she could go with the assurance they could not go far, but by their twelfth day they could all walk and they were up to mischief from the first moment they could leave the den. They seemed totally unaware of the dangers surrounding them, and played in the open where all manner of predators could have snatched them – both from the air and on the ground. Time and again, Masa had to usher them back inside, and time and again they would emerge, testing her patience continually.

However, their cave had been once the lair of a female leopard. When she had spotted the lion approaching during the big storm she had made herself scarce, but now she had come sniffing around. She wanted her home back and, with a leopard about, the lion cubs were in grave danger. So, when Masa found a half-eaten gazelle in a tree not more than a few hundred metres away, she was immediately alert. She ran back quickly to the den site, fearing the worst, but when she made her deep, soft contact call the cubs ran from the cave and gathered around her, all four of them . . . but it was time to move.

By changing the location of their den sites, Masa and her cubs were less likely to attract large predators, especially leopards, hyenas and other lions. They could return again to the same place, but only if they let their own lion smell dissipate first. They did this by moving regularly, minimising the danger that their smell would give away. So, one at a time, Masa picked up the cubs by the scruff of the neck and carried them to the new site she had found. It was another shallow crevice in the rock a few hundred metres further along the crater wall, but it was far enough from the leopard mother and the danger she represented. Each cat had a healthy respect for the other, so they were unlikely to go out of their way to cause trouble, although there was one time when they did cross paths.

The leopard lay on a branch in a large fig tree down by the river. From her vantage point, she could see for many kilometres around, so potential prey could be spotted when it was still some distance away, and by late afternoon a herd of wildebeest was gathering just a kilometre away. It was heading slowly for her part of the river. When their distinctive grunts became audible, she committed to a hunt. It was time for her to come down and take up her ambush position by the riverbank.

Masa and her cubs were nowhere to be seen. She had a clear run. The wildebeest were grazing on fresh grass on the embankment, so the leopard hid behind a croton thicket. Masa, however, was peering out from thick scrub on the opposite bank. She had also spotted the potential for a kill, but had not seen the leopard. They were both unaware of each other's presence.

The wildebeest had made the decision to drink and the first animals were in the water, the rest of the herd following close behind. But just as they lowered their heads to drink, the leopard burst from the bushes on the far bank. The wildebeest panicked and were fleeing in all directions. Masa, who had also identified a target and was starting her run, was startled by the sudden stampede. The leopard saw the lioness and made for the nearest tree. Masa, meanwhile, ignored the animals tripping and falling about her and chased a wildebeest to the top of the embankment. But just as she was about to leap on to her victim, the wildebeest turned abruptly and confronted her. She stopped, and in the heat of the moment turned and ran back a few paces. The wildebeest escaped. Neither cat had made a kill that day, and the wildebeest would not be back for quite a while. Masa sauntered back to her cubs empty-handed, leaving the leopard up the tree.

By now the cubs were 25 days old, and they could run so Masa led them rather than carried them to new campsites. They were four very different characters. Mbili was the thoughtful one, Moja the brave one. Nne was more reserved than the others, while Tatu was . . . well, just Tatu, always up to something. On one journey, their first on to the crater floor, the family passed a flock of guinea fowl in the long grass. They were not worth hunting so Masa left them to their foraging, but not Tatu. He immediately chased the birds, only to be reprimanded with a cuff from his mother for running away, especially when they were out in the open. It was dangerous. They carried on down the slope, away from the safety of the rocks.

They had started out in the twilight just before dawn. It was a cool, crisp morning. The stars were still dimly visible, and the dawn chorus was imminent. First up was a white-browed robin-chat, followed by black-headed orioles down by the river. A pair of boubous interwove their sparkling duet so they sounded as one, and then came the most evocative sound of Africa. The lions of the Lakeside Pride began to roar. It started with a male solo, a low-pitched and throaty roar – an extraordinary sound, which reverberated around the crater. It was felt deep inside rather than heard, a primeval sound that set air and body vibrating.

Masa stopped and listened as other lions joined in; first the other pride male and then the females too. The chorus was almost overwhelming, but it did mean that the pride was clearly some way off and not an immediate threat to her family. She pressed on to find a suitable hiding place. At that moment, other more distant males from other parts of the crater replied to the Lakeside Pride's proclamation. As the eastern rim of the crater lightened the roaring reached a crescendo and then there was a moment of silence. All the birds seemed to be taken unawares, and a few seconds elapsed before they began to pipe up again, the cooing of doves and the croaking of francolins joining the chorus of songbirds in the yellow-barked acacia forest.

Masa stood near the entrance of the new refuge, a hollow in thick vegetation, when out from under a low bush came the four little cubs. They bit her legs and chased her tail, and played rough-and-tumble between themselves. They were still little balls of tawny-coloured fluff, extremely vulnerable and dependent entirely on their mother. She had been moving den sites every few days, surviving on what could be caught on the crater slopes, but now they were on the crater floor she could probably hunt more successfully.

But she was a single mother, without the support of a pride. She would have to hunt alone, feed well to provide milk and later meat for her offspring. Already their milk teeth were pushing through so they could soon try their first solid food. The pressure to deliver would only increase. She also had to protect them from all the dangers on the crater floor. It was a tall order, for this was an exceedingly hostile place, but Masa was no ordinary lioness.

She was tested almost as soon as they arrived, for the den was not as safe as she thought. A herd of buffalo was heading slowly but surely towards the place where she had hidden the cubs. They had been drawn to the fresh, green grass growing there and were unaware that a lion family was laying low just 20 metres away. A large bull raised his head, sniffed the air. He had caught a whiff of something untoward, but seemed unsure what.

One of the cubs climbed out of the ditch in which they were hiding and took a long and somewhat foolish look at the visitors. It was the impetuous Tatu. If the buffalo spotted him he would be a goner, but having satisfied his curiosity, he crawled back down. His mother was barely breathing, lest it gave them away. Thankfully the cubs remained still for the first time in their lives.

The nearest buffalo shook his head, his nostrils flared. He had smelled lion and was immediately ready to act. He stood and searched the undergrowth, but the family was well hidden. A second buffalo raised its head and was testing the air. It grunted. The two stood side by side, the massive bosses across their foreheads and their menacing upturned horns ready to pulverise or gore to death anything that they disliked, and there was little love lost between buffalo and lions.

The two buffalo turned and continued to feed. The lions did not move. Slowly, the herd began to move out of the copse, but the last to leave stopped and sniffed. One of the cubs moved, causing a dry stalk to crack. It was barely audible, but the buffalo had heard it. He walked back to where the cubs were hidden, sniffed again, then thought better of it and went to join the rest of the herd. The cubs were safe for the time being, but what was already becoming clear was that this family, without the protection of a pride, was not going to have an easy ride; and there were to be other scares that day. Living on the crater floor may have enhanced Masa's chances of catching food, but it undoubtedly increased the dangers as well. The second worry was another lion.

It was a male – a solitary nomad. Like Masa, he was taking a chance to be at the heart of the Lakeside Pride territory, but more importantly he was a serious threat to her cubs. As he was not their father, he would have no compunction in killing them. He approached the thicket in which the family was hiding. He had already spotted the mother, but he was cautious. He looked around for signs of a pride. He would do nothing until he was sure that the lioness was alone.

He moved through the long, brown grass, raised his head, grimaced by curling his upper lip and 'tasted' the air – the so-called flehmen response, more usually seen when a male checks out whether a female is on heat, but also adopted when sniffing traces of any interesting smell. He also listened carefully for any hint of other lions, and his body language indicated that he would be taking a special interest in the lone mother.

Two of the cubs ran into the long grass, and began calling. They should have remained hidden, but their insatiable curiosity was getting the better of them. The lion's ears twitched. There were cubs. The only way he could bring this female into oestrus was to kill the cubs, but she was unlikely to let him do that. He moved forward cautiously, disturbing a pair of go-away birds, each with its crest erect. They flew from the bush. The lion was startled momentarily and looked up. Satisfied that it was nothing, he continued to stalk the lioness and her cubs. He sniffed the ground, edging deeper into the vegetation, gradually closer to the place where the cubs were hiding. He pushed forward as if stalking prey, one foot placed carefully in front of the other, his lips taut and his eyes fixed a few metres ahead.

Without warning, Masa burst from the thicket with a full-on attack, but he reeled back as she lunged forward. They growled and snarled ferociously, and she leaped on top of him, sinking her claws and teeth into his rump. He fled, leaping over some rocks, with the lioness directly behind him. She did not let up. Each time she caught him, she gauged and clawed at him, keeping him running. She had to get him as far away from her cubs as she possibly could. She was much smaller than he was, but she had had the element of surprise and she used it to great effect. The male would not return in a hurry. Now she had to move the cubs to a safer place.

Masa returned to the ditch and called. Mbili at least was safe, but the lion had got to Nne before her mother had attacked. She was injured. Tatu and Moja were missing. Their mother led the way out of the ditch and away from the attack site. The two cubs followed, except that the wounded Nne could barely stand on one of her front legs. There was a deep wound where it joined the body and she was limping badly. She could barely keep up. Masa stopped and waited for her, before turning to resume the trek. They had to get to a new refuge, and quickly.

The new site was a cutting in the side of a grassy bank at the side of a dried-out creek or lugga. It was like a natural amphitheatre, so the cubs could not be seen from any predators approaching from three sides. Only the side facing the creek was open, but a ditch to one side could be used if danger should come from this direction. The injured cub collapsed, her brother nuzzling her face, urging her to get up and play; but she remained on her side, exhausted.

With two of her cubs safely at the new site, Masa set off to see if she could locate the other two. It was a long trek and the sun was high in the sky, but she was unwavering. Suddenly, she pulled up. She had seen movement in the grass ahead. She crouched, when out came a serval, a small, spotted cat with large, pointed ears more usually seen at night, but here it was out in the open in the middle of the day. Masa did not move. She did not want draw attention to herself so she let it go unmolested, then continued on to the old rest site.

She called – a gentle, guttural roar, but there was no reply. She searched the undergrowth, but there was no movement. Swarms of flies crowded around her face and got into her eyes, but she was not giving up. She paced to and fro, listening, watching for the slightest sign that her other cubs were here. She wandered in and around the thicket in which she had left them. She would not give up. She grimaced, like the male had done, testing the air for the scent of something familiar. There was a hint of lion cub, but none appeared.

Masa returned to the other cubs, but when she arrived only one came to greet her. She sniffed around and there lying on her side on the bare earth was Nne. She was already dead. Masa licked the lifeless body, while Mbili urged it to play, little understanding that it could not.

An hour passed and the grieving mother eventually abandoned the body. Leaving her surviving cub alone at the creek, she returned yet again to where the lion attack had taken place. She had still not given up on her two missing cubs. She would search for a second time. She called and, suddenly, there they were. They were alive and well. They ran up to her, rubbed heads in greeting and jumped all over her, but she had no time to linger. She immediately gathered them to her and they struck out across the grassland to the lugga where Mbili was waiting. Licking each of them in turn she laid on her side and the surviving cubs drank as if their lives depended on it, which, in a way, they did.

By late afternoon, they were on the move again. They were out in the open, searching for another safe place to rest. It was another lengthy trek, and the cubs with their little legs could barely keep pace with their mother. Nevertheless, they made good time and were closing in on a patch of trees that had been a favourite resting place for the Lakeside Pride. They were nowhere to be seen, so the mother settled her cubs underneath a fallen tree and then left them to go hunting.

Her first encounter was with a mixed herd of wildebeest and zebra, and the grass was so long that she could get to within a few metres of them without being seen. She watched each of animals nearest to her, looking for signs of injury, sickness or a young calf or foal. There was none close to, but across the other side of a stand of trees was a wildebeest with a distinct limp. She made the decision. She had her target. Now, all she had to do was to get to the other side of a herd that was most likely to stampede and bring it down.

She broke from cover and started to run. The wildebeest scattered, the zebra stallions called in alarm. It was bedlam, but the lioness ran through the herd, right through the woods, around a low bush and intercepted her quarry on the other side. She wrapped her forelegs around its neck, and hung there like a giant necklace. She quickly placed her mouth over its mouth and nostrils and suffocated the poor beast. As its body was denied vital life-giving oxygen, the wildebeest crumpled and toppled. In seconds it was dead. What Masa had not realised, however, was that Hasimu and the rest of the Lakeside Pride were no more than a few hundred metres away, resting in the shade of some trees. They were flat out and sound asleep, ignoring the commotion on their doorstep. However, one of the males looked up and saw the young lioness. He just looked and did nothing. The others seemed to be still fast asleep. She looked at him. He looked back, and then she slunk away before the others were roused; but actually it was already too late.

One of the lionesses had stirred and was making a beeline for Masa. It was Hasimu and the way she moved said 'aggression', loud and clear. One of the pride males was on his feet and watched. He roared and this set off the other lionesses. They were all roaring, like a crowd of spectators cheering on their favourite athlete, except this was a matter of life and death.

Masa kept ahead of Hasimu, but the normally lazy lioness had surprising stamina. Wildebeest and zebra stood and stared as the two raced past them, but when Masa was well clear of the pride she stopped suddenly and turned on Hasimu. The older lioness halted abruptly, and realising she had been the only one to give chase, she turned and ran back to the pride. Masa sat panting for a short while. She waited to see if any of the others would appear, before walking back slowly to where she had left the cubs. She stayed with them for an hour or so; long enough for them to get their milk ration, and having lost her wildebeest kill to the pride, she set off to find some other food.

A pair of warthogs scampered away, but they had already seen her so pursuit would have been a waste of time. Next she came face to face with a female waterbuck, but she was not ready to attack and it escaped without it even having to hurry. Then, two male lions appeared, not from the Lakeside Pride – they were busy eating Masa's wildebeest – but more nomads on the lookout for opportunities to take over a pride. She flattened herself against the ground, hoping they had not seen her, but they were already heading in her direction. She looked around for an escape route, but the movement caught their eye. They lowered their heads and approached her, tight-lipped and ready to cause trouble.

About five metres away they stopped, unsure whether to attack. They looked at each other for reassurance, briefly rubbed heads, and then lunged at her. She leaped up and ran like the wind. They gave chase, but she had already made ground and was way ahead of them. The sleeker lionesses are generally faster than males with their large heads and bulky manes. But they were not going to give up so easily. Masa had to run for her life.

She made for the river, and ran along the bank until she found thick cover. The males split up and began to search in and around every bush. After several minutes, they converged on a point overlooking the river and looked down intently. The river was in flood. It was impossible to cross. Instead Masa scrambled part way down a crumbling and almost vertical cliff face and clung to a ledge. And there she stayed, until the two lions became bored and went away.

Scrambling to the top of the bank was not easy, but with a gargantuan effort she hauled herself up the slope and raced back to where she had left the cubs. They were safe, hiding in a ditch, but hungry. She was greeted enthusiastically, and when they had settled down she was able to nurse her family. They fed greedily for about a half-hour, but their milk supply was in danger of running out if the mother could not feed. The next couple of days were critical. Many lion cubs die of starvation, the most common form of mortality for this species. For now, though, they were falling asleep as they suckled. It had been a very scary day.

The following morning Masa, together with Moja, Mbil and Tatu, were on the move again. Masa was desperate to find a good hiding place, away from the Lakeside Pride lionesses and safe from hyenas. This time she was heading for the marsh. She found it easy to hop from one tuft of grass to another, but for the cubs it was a major assault course, especially crossing narrow ditches filled with water. Their little legs were not long enough, and at almost every jump at least one of them received a dunking. Mother hauled them out by the scruff of the neck. They were all wet through, but it did not stop Tatu from being his usual inquisitive self.

He came across a great, grey thing lying in the water and immediately went to investigate. Little did he know it was a hippo, and it could kill a full-grown lioness with one bite of its massive jaws, let alone a small cub. His mother ran up, ready to defend him. The hippo raised his head, but that was all that was needed to put Tatu to flight. His mother backed off slowly, and he stopped to look back at the strange beast, then the four of them headed into the heart of the swamp.

Over the next few days, walking back and forth through the marsh, the cubs quickly learned how to swim. They may have been cats, but they came to be quite unafraid of water. Negotiating this watery world became second nature to them, and the safest place for Masa to hide her cubs was a dense patch of reeds, and that's precisely where she left them when she went hunting.

Creeping out of the reeds, Masa began to stalk a group of wildebeest and zebra. She walked, almost crawled, her body and head low, with just the movement of her shoulder blades visible above the grass. She then lay down as she watched several lines of animals filing past. The place was crawling with them. They were grazing, but also moving slowly towards a patch of open water at the edge of the marsh where they would probably drink. The lioness had to wait. There was a wide expanse of open ground between her and the herd. If she ran too soon, they would all get away.

A zebra stallion strolled away from the herd. She kept her head down. Zebras tend to be more observant than wildebeest and might have given her away. She had to be patient, wait for just the right moment. But the zebra had already spotted her slight movement. He stood not more than a couple of metres from her looking intently at her hiding place. She froze. He could see her back, but he had yet to link the line of beige fur with a predator. He stared, she remained motionless, but when he turned and was about to give the alarm call she erupted from cover. He had forced her hand, but now she had to make the best of it. She had already picked a target and made straight for her quarry. She ran through the wet, marshy ground, but hit a pocket of water and tripped. She recovered quickly and was up and close to her victim. Sensing somehow that it was the target, it stopped and turned to face its executioner. It lunged but the lioness was at its throat in an instant. She wrestled it to the ground, maintaining her bite. It was suffocated in a few minutes.

The ground around the kill was particularly sodden, so she had difficulty in walking around, but after consuming a few mouthfuls of meat she disappeared into the reeds to fetch the cubs. They were about five weeks old, the time when mothers normally introduce cubs to kills. A short while later, she returned to the kill, but she hesitated at the edge of the reeds, making sure that nothing had been attracted to the carcass. Then, all three cubs emerged. The family was together again. They were wet and muddy, but they romped and played before settling down to their next big challenge – meat.

Mother was carefully slicing through the zebra's skin to get at the meat below. Mbili and Tatu watched from a safe distance, hiding from the strange thing that their mother had brought home. Now they were confronted with a kill, the cubs did not know what to make of it. It was the first meat they had seen close up and, at first, they were reluctant to go anywhere near it. The two cubs looked at the carcass, then looked at each other. Neither would dare to go closer. They stared, their eyes popping out of their heads. This was something very new. Mbili squeaked at it. It failed to move so, minute by minute, they became that little bit braver.

Tatu, as usual, was the first to pluck up courage. He sniffed, licked, and then tried his first bite, watching and then copying his mother's every move. His tiny teeth, though, failed to make any impression. The zebra's skin was tougher than it looked. Spurred on by Tatu's bravery, Mbili and Moja crept up to the carcass. They sniffed it, jumped back, and hid behind a tuft of grass. They peered out, and seeing Tatu had already mastered the difficult task of slicing off small pieces of meat, they crawled reluctantly to join him. Their mother helped, tearing off the skin and exposing the fresh, red meat. Mbili and Moja copied Tatu, pushing their faces into the strangely elastic stuff and biting for all they were worth. But Mbili was biting with his front teeth and nothing came away. He watched how his mother was eating. She was using her back teeth to slice the meat and her front ones to pull it away. He tried again. This time he sawed the meat with his tiny back teeth and, lo and behold, a small piece came away. He had his first mouthful of zebra meat. He swallowed, and tried again.

Soon, the three siblings had their faces covered with blood, and their little tummies were full. Mother licked them, and then they licked each other. Much of the carcass remained, so Masa began to haul it away in order to hide it under a bush. She stopped for a moment, stared out over the grass, searching carefully for any signs of danger. Her family was vulnerable out here in the open, and it would not be too long before others were attracted to the kill. Already vultures had gathered in the trees and on the ground, and wherever there are vultures, hyenas and jackals, and even lions, were sure to follow. Masa, however, denied them a meal for now. She straddled the remains of the carcass and dragged it into the thick under-growth, where the birds could not reach it. They would return to it later, but for now they had to drink.

Nervously, Masa walked down a path worn bare by the hooves of the local wildebeest. Her cubs waited on a low embankment as she went to the water's edge. She looked up and down the riverbank for signs of other predators. There were none, although they were not alone. Further downstream a pair of giraffes stood with their legs splayed and their long necks bent down to the water. One drank while the other kept lookout. They had nothing to fear from Masa and her family. One kick and she could be very badly injured. Lions had a healthy respect for giraffes. Even so, Mbili could not help staring.

Masa lowered her head to drink but every few laps she looked up quickly to check for danger. She called and the cubs ran down to join her. This was the latest stop on their guided tour. One day, they would have to fend for themselves, so knowing the safe places to eat, drink and rest were vital to their own survival. It was also part of their learning to know when something was real or not. Each time a cub put his head down to drink he bared his teeth and hissed at the image in the water. It would be long while before they got used to seeing themselves every time they drank. But, for now, they had not even learned to lap. They dipped in their paws and licked them instead.

And, in order to cross the stream, they had to discover that if they dallied too long, they would get stuck in the mud. Mother crossed first to show them how it was done and the cubs quickly followed behind her. Safely across, the family walked back on to the grass. With the temperature rising, it was time to rest.

A heron glided down to land next to a pool near the river. Tatu bounded over to look but dared not cross the deeper water. The bird ignored him, focussing all its attention on frogs that were spawning in the warm, shallow water ponds that had formed when the water level dropped. A yellow-billed stork waded through the shallower parts of the main river channel searching for catfish. Bee-eaters perched on twigs close to their nest burrows in the soft riverbank, and a black-and-white pied wagtail flitted across a sandbank. They were catching flies, and there were plenty of those. When Masa raised her head, a cloud engulfed her. They got everywhere – in nostrils, eyes and ears. She shook her head, and lowered it again.

It was hot, but Mbili, Tatu and Moja went exploring all the same, and they had found a new playmate. A young plover was minding its own business, looking for titbits amongst the rocks, when the lion cubs interrupted it. They stalked it, chased it, but instead of flying, it ran away as fast as its little legs would carry it. It seemed to know these three hunters were novices; so it saved its energy. The three cubs eventually gave up. To stalk prey successfully, they should have used at least *some* cover, but it was all a part of learning how to be a lion.

Suddenly, Masa was alert. She had heard the bark of a male baboon. She clambered to the top of the embankment and searched the skyline. There she could see their unmistakeable shapes – the dog-like head, the piercing eyes set close together on the face, and the thick mane, almost like a lion's, of the adult males – and coming down the track was an exceptionally large troop. They were little threat to a full-grown lion, but there were so many animals the cubs could be in danger. She trotted back to where they were playing and led them to a hiding place. As long as they remained quiet and did not move, they should be safe.

A large male was first to cross the water. He waded in and the water was soon up to his belly. Babies hanging underneath their mothers would be getting a dunking. Some of the youngsters leaped from rock to rock, trying but failing to keep their feet dry. When they were on the same side of the river as Masa and her cubs, they spread out and searched amongst the vegetation for anything remotely edible.

Masa stood up and slunk away, hiding below an overhang, ready to attack if necessary, but leaving her youngsters alone in a hollow shielded by thick bushes. They cowered as instinct kicked in. They kept their bodies low to the ground, and were completely silent.

The baboons were scattered all around. Some foraged, others drank, but one large male ventured ever closer to the cubs' hiding place. He had picked up their scent and was looking intently at the spot, but he would not go any further.

He shook the bushes and barked, hoping to drive them out, but the cubs stayed put, and so did their mother. The baboons hung about and drank from the river before moving on. They were more interested in foraging than tormenting lion cubs, unaware that if they had attacked, Masa would have killed many of their number. In a way, *they* had had a lucky escape, as well as the cubs.

When she was sure they had cleared the area, Masa came out from her hideaway and called her cubs, but only Mbili appeared. She called again, but there was no answer. The other cubs had become separated. Where was Tatu? Masa searched the thick vegetation, calling continuously; and then she heard a familiar bleat, and Tatu came tumbling down the rocky slope followed closely by Moja. Tatu called loudly and Mbili ran to fight with him. Maybe it was a lion cub's sign of affection, but he certainly seemed pleased to see his brother and sister. Masa rubbed heads with her three cubs, licking the top of first Tatu's and then Moja's scalp, and the four of them sauntered along the riverbank side-by-side.

After a few hours, the family returned to the remains of the kill, but something – probably a hyena – had pulled it out from beneath the bushes, and left in a hurry when the lioness returned. The vultures were crowded around, squabbling noisily. One after the other, they plunged their naked and blood-splattered heads and necks into the carcass and pulled out morsels of meat and guts. They chattered constantly and stretched their wings, each trying to dominate its neighbour and take the best of the leftovers.

As the cubs watched from a safe distance, the lioness lowered her head, put back her ears, and ran straight at the crowd. They flew up, but one was not quick enough. Masa caught it with her paw and brought it down. The vulture, though, instinctively played dead. It remained quite motionless and Masa was unsure what to do. It did not smell interesting and it did not struggle. She walked around it, and pawed it cautiously. Still the vulture did not move. In the end, she let it be, turning her attention to what remained of the wildebeest. With her back turned, the vulture flapped erratically into the air and was gone. Its survival strategy had worked.

The rest of the birds, though, were still gathered around, and a group of jackals had joined the fray. They fussed about, darting in to grab a mouthful while Masa called for the cubs, but for the little ones it was all rather intimidating for they had to run a gauntlet of jackals and vultures. They felt vulnerable in the presence of so many, and scavengers could become predators in an instant. Mbili and Moja kept close to Masa, but Tatu dawdled and was inadvertently left behind. A jackal circled him menacingly. The cub bristled and bleated. More jackals circled. They had left the kill to Masa, Moja and Mbili and were now focussing on easier meat. Tatu was in trouble. He ran at the jackals with his mouth open and his tiny teeth bared in defiance, and they jumped back, but he was not going to keep them off for long. His tormentors ran back and forth in front of him, looking for a weak point, but really not knowing how to tackle such a little fighter. Then he marched determinedly towards his mother. The jackals seemed to be taken aback and none came forward to harm him. He had saved himself by his own determination. He had earned his place at the table.

A kill like this, which lasted Masa for several days, had to be a regular occurrence. With growing cubs, as well as her own appetite, to satisfy, she had to be catching prey regularly. It also meant that she had to leave the cubs for long periods, and the longer they were alone, the more likely they were to be exposed to all the hazards of the crater. Sometimes a series of seemingly innocuous events conspired to put them at most risk.

And so it was one bright day in the crater. The Lakeside Pride had decamped to a rest site not far from the cubs' hiding place, but as long as they remained out of sight and avoided attracing attention they were relatively safe. All the members of the pride were relaxed, enjoying their daily nap, when a couple of elephants were on their doorstep. The pride had not noticed their silent approach, but now the lions had to move or risk being trampled. They quickly got up and moved out of the way. But the elephants had driven them towards the place where the three cubs were hidden.

The lions quickly found them and surrounded them, sniffing and pawing. The pride's own slightly older cubs were especially inquisitive, touching the younger cubs and causing them to turn submissively on to their backs. The adults pushed their own youngsters out of the way, and sniffed at the three outsiders. Masa's cubs, in turn, bit and scratched as best they could, but were frightened as each and every member of the pride came to see who they were. Would they accept them or would they kill them? It would only take one lion to take umbrage, and the cubs were dead.

Without warning, however, the pride suddenly abandoned the three cubs. They just walked off and left them. Mbili, Tatu and Moja were unharmed, but they were now out in the open, where all manner of other predators might spot them. Their mother was somewhere else stalking an eland family so, chastened by their encounter with the Lakeside Pride, Mbili took the initiative and, following his lead, the three cubs set out by themselves through the open grassland in search of a less conspicuous place to hide . . . but they had already been spotted.

A martial eagle soared high overhead, and circled. It was nearly 300 metres up, but it had such keen eyesight, it had seen the movement of the youngsters in the grass. It was a big bird. With a wingspan of over nearly two metres, making it the largest and the most powerful eagle in Africa. It could pluck a small antelope from the savannah and lift it aloft, so a lion cub would be an easy catch. It spiralled down slowly, always keeping the cubs in view. It would stoop sharply to catch its prey, but it was waiting for just the right moment. The cubs, however, were blissfully unaware of any danger from above. They ploughed on through the grass. The eagle descended steadily, and then suddenly swooped. Mbili saw movement out of the corner of his eye. He snarled – more a bleat that a snarl, but it worked. As he dived for the cover of a fallen branch, the other cubs ran. They both scampered beneath a low bush. The eagle missed all of them, but it landed nearby and hopped over to where Mbili was hiding. Before it reached the cub, Mbili ran and joined his siblings in the thick undergrowth. They were safer there. The eagle hopped about, peering below the bush, frustrated that it could not winkle them out. It took off and left to hunt easier prey.

The cubs were visibly shaken up. This was a whole new experience – this danger from the sky. They did not have the courage to move for quite a while, but their hiding place was not ideal. One by one, they poked out their noses, tested the air, and started out again. Mbili had noticed some trees that were not that far away. They would look there for a safe place to hide.

As they walked, swallows swooped low over their heads. The cubs cowered at first, but soon realised that these small birds were harmless. They had travelled all the way from southern Turkey to be here and they were hawking for insects, especially the flies that were following the cubs. They were joined by a flycatcher that dropped on to the ground in front of them, then darted up to catch its prey.

Those precious moments of tranquillity, however, were short-lived. Lying on the ground directly ahead was a hyena. It was sprawled out on its side in the sun. Mbili almost walked into it, but stopped just in time. He backed away, right into Tatu who was directly behind him, forcing Moja to stop too. The three cubs remained remarkably still for a while. Fortunately, the hyena had not heard them, so when they thought it safe, they began a detour. With long grass as their cover, they crawled on their bellies towards the trees. The hyena stirred. They stopped and waited for it to settle again before moving on, but by crawling as flat as they could, their progress was painfully slow. The hyena moved again. This time it raised itself on to its forelegs. It had picked up the smell of lion and was looking all around, but it could see nothing.

The three cubs stopped. The hyena stood on all fours, its thick neck erect. Again, it looked around. Still nothing. It was just about to settle back down, when Moja snapped a dry grass stem. The sound seemed almost deafening. The hyena leapt up, lunged forward and grabbed the cub in its powerful jaws. Mbili and Tatu ran for all they were worth, but Moja was killed with the first bite. The hyena walked back to its resting place to eat its bloody meal.

The two surviving cubs were still running, but before they could reach the trees, the hyena spotted them. It left the body of the young cub and made after Mbili and Tatu. For every five or six strides they made it only had to make one. It was gaining on them. Mbili hesitated and looked back, but seeing the hyena approaching made him redouble his pace. Tatu made straight for a hollow at the base of a large fig tree, Mbili not far behind. Tatu scrambled in, followed by Mbili, and not a moment too soon. The hyena gnashed at Mbili, but caught only air. The two cubs pushed as far as they could to the back of the hollow, their bodies trembling with fear. If only their mother would come, then it would be all right, but she was nowhere to be seen. Now, there were only the two brothers left and they were very much on their own.

The two surviving cubs eventually gained enough courage to peek out of their hideaway. The hyena had gone. Mbili took a step outside. Nothing untoward happened. Nothing swooped down from the sky, nothing came out from behind a tree, and nothing ran at them from across the grass. Gaining confidence, he took another step. Still nothing happened. Half his body was out of the tree hollow, when there was an almighty crash and his world lit up. A storm. Mbili dashed back inside. He was not as brave as he thought. He pushed up against Tatu, burying his head in Tatu's fur, trying as best he could to be as far away as possible from such a frightening thing. His legs shook, and he began to pant. Another crash and a deep rumble, and then came the rain. A deluge. The cubs, however, were safe and dry. Tatu ventured to the entrance of the hollow and peered out as Mbili had done. Lightning arced down from the sky and seconds later the ground seemed to shake. Wind drove the rain in great waves across the sky. And then it had passed; the squall had stopped just as suddenly as it had started. The sun came out and the grass glistened.

Masa was quite unaware of the drama acting out not more than a kilometre away. She was hunting when the storm was approaching, Masa had spotted a lone Thomson's gazelle. From her slightly elevated position she could see the dark clouds approaching and the forks of lightening darting to the ground. The gazelle seemed unperturbed and continued to graze. Masa made her way swiftly through the long grass towards her intended victim. Every time the gazelle looked up she stopped, and every time he put his head down to eat, she moved forward until she was little more than ten metres away, then stopped again. As thunder rumbled, she sat back on her haunches, and remained absolutely still, trying to figure out what to do next. The gazelle was unaware that she was there. The next time he looked up he looked directly at her but did not see her. As his head went down, she edged slowly forwards, ready to run should she have to.

The gazelle had bulging eyes at the side of its head giving it excellent front and sideways vision, so the cat had to wait until it turned its back and she was in its blind spot before making a move. Then the storm broke and the rain came down. Against all odds, the gazelle stopped eating and sat down. Its hind legs, however, were bunched ready to launch it straight up into the air and away should danger threaten. The lioness's legs were equally ready, but she had to judge the right moment to launch her attack.

The seconds ticked by, and then minutes, and still neither lioness nor gazelle had moved. She was soaked to the skin but she was ready to charge. Step by step she inched forward, her head and eyes locked on to the prey. The gazelle looked away and began to nibble its legs. It was the moment she had been waiting for. She moved, slowly at first, and then accelerated rapidly. For a split second the gazelle did not see her, but then turned, saw the movement and exploded into life. With the gazelle just a few metres ahead of the lioness, they ran in a wide arc, but the gazelle pulled a very tight turn leaving Masa to continue on the same course. She slowed to a stop. There was no point in chasing. She had lost the element of surprise. The hunt had failed and she was drenched. She sauntered over to a low tree, flopped down and waited for the rain to stop.

A small herd of buffalo were undisturbed by the bright flashes and thunderous booms. Intent on feeding come what may, they continued to graze as if nothing untoward was happening; yet, less than 500 metres away trees were thrashing about in the storm and lightning tore one asunder. But, as the storm moved on, the dark curtains of falling rain parted to reveal the red clouds of an African dusk. One by one the buffalo looked up, the boss of their wet horns reflecting the last light of the sun.

The two cubs, meanwhile, had ventured out of their hole. In the fading light, Mbili had spotted a grasshopper on a grass stem and immediately did what should come naturally to a lion: he started to stalk. He may have been small but he seemed to know what to do. He moved slowly and deliberately, placing one foot deftly in front of the other, pausing if the grasshopper looked as if it was about to escape and inching forward when it was still. He bunched up his muscles, just as he had seen his mother do, and pounced. He landed right on top of the unfortunate insect and flattened it against the ground. He bit into its juicy abdomen and, hey presto – he had caught his first meal all by himself. Tatu came to join him, and they romped about as if nothing momentous had happened.

Masa, however, had returned to their previous den site, but she could not see her babies. She searched high and low around the place where she had last left them, but the cubs had gone. Despite the rain, the smell of lions lingered. The Lakeside Pride had been there. Had they killed her cubs? She called for them with a quiet roar, careful not to alert the other lions. She felt hot and flustered, her damp face covered with an irritating swarm of biting flies. She called some more. Again, there was nothing. She searched all over the area. No cubs. She looked about her, and saw the silhouette of trees. Could they have hidden there? She walked slowly, checking that nothing was following her. As darkness fell, she walked towards the hollow tree and called, and out popped Mbili and Tatu from inside. But there was no Moja. Masa feared the worst. She looked all around the area, discovered drops of blood on the ground and the smell of hyena all around. She knew it was of no use to look any further. Another cub was dead.

But Mbili and Tatu were safe. They had been hiding in the best place for miles around, and had made it there all by themselves. These two were proving to be cleverer than the average lion cub. They were born survivors – two survivors from a litter of four. The brothers ran to their mother and were greeted with a fusillade of head rubbing and licking, and a very welcome bellyful of milk.

CHAPTER THREE

– Survival School –

While she brought up the two brothers, Masa remained in touch with the Lakeside Pride, always with the vain hope that some day she might be accepted back into the group, but she was never allowed. Hasimu saw to that. Masa made contact with the pride males occasionally, and they did not attack her, but as soon as Hasimu knew she was there, the older lioness made sure that the others ganged up on the outcast and she was chased away mercilessly. Masa had to ensure that she and her family were always at least a kilometre away from the pride, but from time to time she kept in visual contact, just in case there was a change of heart.

Her surviving cubs – Mbili and Tatu – played around her with endless rough and tumble games and stalking practice. They were growing fast, stronger and more mobile. They were taking an interest in the movement and behaviour of prey and were beginning to watch Masa when she went hunting. Their chances of survival were increasing day by day, and the two cubs were finding that sometimes it was the little things that commanded their attention as well as the big ones.

And so it was one fine day that Masa and her two cubs were sprawled around a fallen tree, its bare branches and the arch of the fallen trunk giving them some shade from the sun. All was quiet. Even the cubs were subdued. It seemed a good place to rest, for from here Masa could see over the grassland and observe any animals that were heading for the river to drink. Lions are basically lazy predators, quite happy to let the prey come to them, rather than them having to go to the prey. So, it was here that they would have spent the remainder of the day, except there was a small problem, an insect-sized problem, for the log was also home to less tolerant creatures – bees.

African honeybees are especially aggressive, and this colony was no exception. The bees streamed from their nest and the swarm gathered around the lions. They shook their heads and pawed at the insects to no effect. The bees were unhappy with their new neighbours and they were showing it. Mbili sneezed, the result of a painful sting on his nose. The others snarled and growled, but it was all to no avail. The bees pressed home their attack. They wanted the lions out of there, and one by one the family was forced to move away, abandoning the fallen tree to its rightful residents. The bees had won.

Masa led the way, with the brothers close behind. The bees followed them for nearly half a kilometre before they broke away and flew back to their nest. It had been a painful lesson for Mbili and Tatu. They would certainly avoid those little characters in future. They carried on, but were walking from the frying pan into the fire.

Ahead of the three lions was a herd of domestic cattle, tended by several young boys. They were all heading for the river to drink, but Masa and the two brothers were in their way. The moment they spotted the lions, they shouted and waved sticks. Masa began to take a detour, but out from behind a thicket came a gang of older herdsmen – warriors brandishing spears. They saw the lone lioness as a threat and began to give chase.

Masa ran, but the young cubs could barely keep up. She looked around desperately for somewhere they could hide. Then she spotted a large burrow. It was an old warthog tunnel. It had partially collapsed but there was just enough room for the two young lions. She guided them in, made sure they were secure, and ran again, hopefully drawing the herdsmen away by running in a wide arc.

The men came to halt directly next to the burrow's entrance. Unlike a hyena or lion, the men could not smell the lion cubs, and Mbili and Tatu remained very still. They could hear the men talking excitedly. They were standing and pointing at Masa, but they had given up the chase. One man took his spear and prodded down the tunnel, more out of curiosity than expecting to spear a lion. The tip missed Tatu by centimetres, but still he did not move. In fact, he was hardly breathing.

Gradually the voices became fainter, and the tinkle of cowbells receded into the distance. The men and their cattle were going away. Masa doubled back and called to the cubs. They ran out of the burrow and jumped all over their mother. With the temperature soaring again, however, the family needed to find shade. They headed for a stand of trees on a hillock, but to get to it they had to cross a stream. Masa leaped across with considerable ease, but for the cubs it was a chasm. They watched their mother, and then tried themselves. They both made it across, but they could not quite make it and keep dry . . . each had a wet behind.

As they made their way, the sky darkened to a deep indigo, and the brown grass almost glowed in the afternoon sun. As distant thunder rumbled and lightning forks zigzagged across the eastern sky, the wildebeest began to bunch together. There was more rain coming. The sky turned from dark blue to black, and anything on the flat grassland was starkly outlined. With the temperature dropping, it was an ideal time for hunting but a lioness from the Lakeside Pride had the same idea and by coincidence was stalking the same prey as Masa. They were on a collision course and neither knew the other was there.

The target was a lone wildebeest and, as both lionesses approached from opposite directions, it did not flee. The poor animal had a broken leg. It simply stood and waited for the inevitable. Masa was just about to charge it when, just in time, she spotted the Lakeside lioness. She eased back silently into the long grass and watched. Being faced with an animal that did not run away, however, was somewhat unnerving for the other lioness. Instead of charging, she walked around her intended victim. At the last minute the wildebeest tried to escape, but that was what she had been waiting for. She grabbed its throat and pulled it over. It was the easiest kill she had had for many a year. Before the wildebeest was dead, another lioness from the Lakeside Pride arrived, followed by several more. Masa looked on from a short distance away, but the lionesses were so preoccupied they failed to see her. She gathered her youngsters to her and made quick her escape. At that moment the heavens opened.

As the rain lashed down and visibility dropped, the family strolled on down to the marsh. They sat beside a large pool covered in floating weed, and the cubs watched a flock of jacanas striding over the top with their outsized feet. It looked to all the world as if the weed was solid ground, but the irrepressible Tatu was about to discover the awful truth. He leapt straight on to the weed and to his great surprise found himself not on dry land but under the water. He bobbed to the surface and gasped for air, dog-paddling frantically to keep himself afloat. He grabbed the overhanging vegetation and tried desperately to haul himself back up the steep bank.

A hippo suddenly popped his head up through the weeds. His afternoon siesta had been rudely interrupted, but before he could admonish the culprit, the little cub had hauled himself back on to the bank. The others, including his very concerned mother, joined the little drowned rat, sniffing him, licking him and rubbing his head. It was an experience he would probably not want to repeat. They all made a hasty retreat.

When the rain had ceased, the family walked along the river, crossing a small beach before stopping at the water's edge. There, Masa crouched to drink. The cubs joined her, no longer fearful of their own reflections. Tatu broke off and stalked a wader that had been foraging in the shallow water. Every day the cubs were honing the skills they would need to survive when they became adults. Mbili pursued a butterfly, while Tatu left the bird and began to stalk his brother, bringing him down in another game of predator and prey. Their mother climbed up the riverbank and settled down in the shade. The little ones followed, clambering up the bank with ease. They were becoming stronger every minute, but they were still vulnerable.

On the beach below, the first visitor was not a predator but a large male waterbuck. It had come down to the river to drink, and was quite unaware that a family of lions was directly behind him. He dipped his head to drink, while one of the cubs looked down, mesmerised by the mysterious beast. When it had gone Masa encouraged the cubs to move on. She tried to grab Tatu by the nape and, even though he was quite capable of getting down himself, tried to carry him down the bank. Tatu kicked and struggled. He was certainly not going to be carried any more. It was another sign that the cubs were growing up. Mbili came close behind, and they settled on a mound with a view across the surrounding grassland.

Masa lay down while the cubs played their usual game of tag

and tumble, but they were brought up short when a party of three ground hornbills appeared. They were walking and hopping through the grass searching for insects and other food. Masa ignored them. They were not food for her. The brothers, though, were intrigued. These birds may not have represented a meal, but chasing them would certainly be fun. Mbili immediately went into the stalking position, his body low to the ground, his ears alert. He had been learning well from his mother. The hornbills came closer and one was just a metre away but Mbili's nerve failed at the last moment and he came running back to mother. This strange creature with its black plumage and red head and face was more than a young lion could take. The birds walked on unconcerned; after all, if the youngster had not bottled out, they could just as easily escaped by flying away, and that would have confused the young cubs even more!

Just then a hyena ran into the shallows of the nearby crater lake and scattered the flamingos that lived there. The entire flock with two or three hundred birds rose as one. Mbili and Tatu stopped what they had been doing and looked above them. The noise was deafening, every flamingo calling in alarm. They swooped around the lake in a confusion of white, black and pink, each circuit bringing them gradually down to the surface. A few at the leading edge lowered their long spindly legs and they landed gently in the shallows. The rest of the flock came in behind them, looking, from a distance, as if they were actually running on water. After much wing folding and head turning, they all got down again to the busy task of feeding on the shrimps and algae that thrive in the soda-rich waters.

Masa licked the back of first Mbili's head and then Tatu's, and then rolled on to her back with her paws dangling in the air. Tatu rejoined Mbili and the two cubs pummelled her tummy, and she suckled them – the gentler side of a formidable predator. As she stood up, Mbili and Tatu jumped around her, catching her tail and grappling round her neck. They were growing fast but they were still cubs, and their mother had to leave them in order to go hunting again. They were not yet big or strong enough to join in a hunt, so she left them close to a trench surrounded by high grass. The two cubs continued to play, biting each other's tail, stalking and pouncing, before tiredness got the better of them and they were soon fast asleep.

Masa was sprawled on an old termite mound, when she began to stare out across the plain. Instead of standing on top of the mound to get a better view, as she often did prior to a hunt, she came down and peered around it, careful not to reveal that she was there at all. In the distance she could see a lioness from the Lakeside Pride. It was Hasimu, and she was alone. The older lioness had seen the activity around the mound and had gone to investigate. She crept up slowly and was no more than a few hundred metres away. Masa looked around quickly, looking for an escape route. Her cubs were awake, but they had not noticed the intruder. However, when they saw their mother's change of behaviour they were instantly vigilant.

Hasimu stopped and looked towards the mound. The cubs ran for cover, but Masa kept the intruder in view, almost goading the other lioness to follow her and not her cubs. Hasimu stopped again, as if assessing the situation. As Masa turned, however, her rival trotted forward, and then she began to stalk. She was stalking the cubs. Masa made a low-pitched sound and turned to Mbili and Tatu who were still watching nearby. They responded by running down to the river. Their mother remained where she was. She would try to face off the other lioness as long as she could. The two adversaries faced each other, staring, but neither moving as much as an eyelid.

Masa stepped forward. Hasimu flinched. Masa charged and the intruder turned and fled, Masa right behind her. Hasimu knew that should Masa catch her it could mean serious injury or even death. She kept on running. The cubs were safe, at least, for one more day, or so she thought. As Masa followed the direction in which her cubs had fled, she discovered they were holed up right under the noses of a couple of bull elephants. They had been ambling down to the water, but now they were looking nervous. They had secretions running down the sides of their heads, a sure sign that they were stressed by something, probably the lioness. Masa already had a healthy respect for elephants. They were unpredictable. If they should panic, they could trample the cubs, intentionally or accidentally. One of them raised its trunk, checking the air. It had picked up the smell of lion, and was ready for an attack if it should come. Then one behind the other, they filed away, back on to the open grassland.

When the elephants had gone, Masa emerged from the undergrowth and strolled along the riverbank. She came to the hollow and there were her two cubs. They ran out to greet her, and then chased each other over a sandbank. They were brimming with confidence, but the reality was that these two youngsters were as vulnerable as any others on the plains. They clambered over their mother's sprawling body, pushing their heads against hers, fighting and biting each other all the while. They were now about three months old, so Masa had to provide sufficient meat for the rapidly growing bodies as well as provide them with a top up of milk. Leaving them in this safe place, she went in search of prey.

A half-hour later she was on a small rise, well camouflaged and overlooking a watering hole. She looked out intently, watching for anything that moved, her head supported by her paws and her tail lying loosely behind. Her tan coat blended in perfectly with the dried vegetation, making her almost invisible. From her vantage point, she could see that a few wildebeest were heading for the river and, in order to get there, they had to pass close by – Mother Nature's home delivery service. It was time to set up an ambush. Hiding in the bushes, she waited for a wildebeest to come closer.

By the time she was ready, however, the first few wildebeest had already reached the river. They gathered at the top of the bank, nervous about taking the next step. They stood and stared down at the water. More animals joined the ranks and gradually those at the front were feeling the pressure from those behind, but still they did not move. A small group of zebra pushed to the front. The stallion scanned both banks and the surface of the water and saw nothing untoward. He led his family down a muddy gully. They had to cross the river in order to reach a swathe of lush grass on the other side. While the zebra walked on, the wildebeest hesitated in small, closely bunched groups. Masa positioned herself below an overhang on the riverbank. Long grass and small bushes obscured her from the herd.

The first line of wildebeest began to follow the zebra across, and the urge to move rippled through the herd. Within minutes they were all walking towards a gully that funnelled the animals right next to Masa's hiding place. She just had to wait until an animal of suitable size walked past – one not too big or she would have difficulty bringing it down, and not too small so that she had ample food for a couple of days.

She bunched up her body and positioned her feet carefully, ready to pounce. Suddenly she raced out and into the stream of animals. They panicked. Wildebeest and zebras were running in every direction. Zebras whinnied. Wildebeest snorted. Those coming down the gully turned about and ran back up. Those by the river dashed across. But she managed to grab a young wildebeest by the throat. It struggled, but she hung on tight, her formidable jaws clamped on to the underside of the wildebeest's neck. All around her there was chaos, as wildebeest and zebras clambered around and on top of each other as they tried desperately to make their escape.

In the pandemonium, Masa released her grip, dropped the youngster and leaped out to catch a second one, bringing it down and killing it in seconds. Quickly, she dragged the limp body into a thicket and out of sight. Even with her powerful, vice-like bite, she had been unable to despatch the first target quickly enough, so she had sought a second. Zebra stallions called excitedly and then turned to see what had caused the stampede. They stood firm, eyes and ears focussed on the gully and, as the dust settled, they could see the first of Masa's victims. It staggered to its feet and wandered aimlessly for several metres, before returning to the herd. The lioness had her prey. The other young beast was lucky to be alive.

Having hidden the carcass in thick vegetation, Masa went to fetch the cubs. They stopped for a drink at a puddle, and then crossed a narrow part of the river by using a fallen log. The carcass, however, was at the top of a steep, almost vertical, bank and, try as they might, the two brothers failed to clamber up the crumbling soil. Time after time, they hauled themselves as high as they could, only to fall back down in a cloud of dust and a landslide of pebbles. But they had to reach the top if they were to eat. Mbili found some hanging vegetation and was able haul himself up to the top, but Tatu just kept on trying. Almost exhausted and crying loudly, he finally found a place where the going was firm and he too reached the top, running immediately to his mother, grabbing her neck and rubbing heads. Then she led the two cubs to where she had hidden the food. She hauled out the carcass from under the bush and into the open, and waited.

The two brothers were at a loss. They did not know what to do. Normally their mother would cut the body open so they could reach the juicy meat underneath the tough hide, but it was time for another lesson – what to do with prey once it has been caught. At first they licked and they bit, but they were having little success. Nevertheless, they had to work it out for themselves. Masa left them and went for the shade of a nearby tree, and one of the cubs got the message. Mbili grabbed the wildebeest by the throat and began to haul it towards the shade. It was a considerable weight, and the little fellow pulled and he pulled. Tatu looked on but failed to help. He seemed more interested in playing. But Mbili was not deterred. It took a little while, but he dragged the body towards his mother and she rewarded him by piercing the skin so he could get at the meat below. Tatu quickly joined him, and the family tucked into their evening meal, their bloodstained faces popping up from time to time as if coming up for air.

At the start of the rainy season, life in the crater was buckling under the heat, but the weather was beginning to turn. Humidity was high and there was the prospect of another hefty storm. By midday, billowing clouds obscured the sun. Gloom pushed out the brightness, and distant claps of thunder announced that the storm was brewing. First a few spots, then a deluge swept across the crater floor. The wildebeest, zebra and gazelles simply stopped where they stood, their backs to the wind and lashing rain. It was just what Masa had been waiting for. She emerged quickly from her hideaway and on to the grassland. They were all sitting targets. All she need do was find one that she could capture alone.

She waited for the rain to set in and the wind to drop; then she began to stalk. She was able to come up right behind a gazelle, it did not see her and could not smell her. The grass was just high enough to obscure most of her body, only her shoulders and back visible. The brothers were watching her every move. She started to stalk, but instead of staying back and observing the hunt from a distance they followed her. The gazelle was resting just in front of Masa and had not seen her approach. She bunched up her muscles, ready to charge, but Tatu had not only started to play directly behind her but he was also pulling her tail. She froze. He was going to give the game away. The gazelle got to its feet and looked in their direction. Masa charged, but the gazelle had more than a head start and the lioness knew she would not catch it. After a few strides, she gave up. Tatu's exuberance had cost them a meal.

Duly admonished, Tatu crawled away. Masa tried again. This time a group of male wildebeest had caught her eye. She stalked as close as she dare, but they spotted her immediately. They began to walk towards her rather than flee. She had given herself away and male wildebeest en masse were formidable opponents. Masa walked on, their long, black faces turning to watch her go.

Visibility deteriorated even more and, as the afternoon wore on, the skies filled and the heavens opened once more. The small groups of wildebeest stood shoulder to shoulder and zebra families huddled together. Elephants enjoyed the cool shower, and the hippos in the marsh were in their element. Masa returned to the cubs. They nestled into their mother, but their fur was soaked and flat against their bodies. Mother sat impassively. There was little she could do. This was not just a heavy shower. The three of them were in a full-blown storm. It was time to seek better shelter. The youngsters were beginning to shiver from the cold, and the ground was saturated, with pools and puddles forming everywhere.

They found a gully, with an overhang that protected them from the worst of the weather. They sat it out at first. They had all had a good soaking, but it failed to put the dampers on the cubs' play-time. They were completely drenched, but the more it rained, the more they played, and they had found a new plaything.

A hammerkop, a short fat-billed relative of the tall and slender storks, had put down in the rain to search for frogs and toads, but once Tatu had spotted it, the bird became the unwitting target of hunting practice. Both cubs crouched and stalked, but with its afternoon foray interrupted, the bird flapped unhurriedly into the air and glided to a quieter location a little further on. They went back to rolling in the wet grass, while all around them thunder crashed and lightning flashed. They were no longer afraid of storms. It was all a part of growing up in the crater.

By late afternoon, the rain had cleared for a short time, the sun appeared and life was getting back to normal. The air was fresh, the temperature had dropped, and conditions were clear and crisp like an autumn day in northern Europe. Mother was out hunting so the cubs were on their own, playing close to the marsh and a waterhole containing a bevy of noisy hippos. They usually came out at night, but one or two had come out to crop the grass while the rain was falling and had not returned to the water. The cubs were enthralled at finding more playmates, except these were three-tonne animals with tempers to match. Fortunately the cubs kept their distance, but they watched every move these great beasts made.

As evening approached, however, another deluge hit the area. Rain came down in sheets and the thunder crashed overhead. Masa and her cubs were soaked again but, more alarmingly, the gully in which they were hiding was filling up with water. The small and normally inoffensive river was funnelling floodwater from the crater walls and it was turning into a raging torrent. The cubs were in danger of drowning. Their mother guided them out and they took shelter amongst a stand of acacias nearby. As long as the crater's lions and hyenas were also sheltering from the weather, the cubs should be relatively safe, but should any of the other predators be abroad that night, they were most definitely at risk.

Masa left them amongst the trees. The torrential rain carried on into the night. Most animals on the plains were standing or sitting it out. Gazelles either stood where they had been feeding or sat on the ground, their bodies hunched up and their backs against the wind. The conditions seemed to dampen their vigilance. Distracted by the weather, they were paying less attention to what was going on around them. It was all a big cat could ask for. She moved swiftly from thicket to thicket without being seen, searching for any animals that were sitting rather than standing. They would lose vital seconds in trying to get to their feet, and it could mean the difference between life and death for the prey, and a meal or not for the predator. On this night, it was unfortunately 'not'.

By morning, the rain had stopped and the river level had fallen. Masa returned to the cubs' hiding place, where Mbili leaped on to her back and fell on to the ground. At first, Tatu was nowhere to seen, but after a few minutes he too was centre stage and stalking his mother's tail. He tumbled into her prostrate body and was licked hard all over for his trouble. Mother and both cubs had survived the night.

While Masa watched over them, Mbili and Tatu played stalking and pouncing. They were getting quite good, but their game was interrupted when two giraffes appeared. Faced with the three cats, the giraffes stood and stared. They would not let the lions out of their sight. They towered over Mbili and Tatu, but the two cubs seemed unperturbed by their lofty visitors and started to groom. Eventually the giraffes felt it safe to continue, but every so often they stopped, turned and looked around just in case they were being followed. But there was more accessible prey in the offing and Masa was following its every move.

As the day wore on, wildebeest began to gather by the river for their daily drink. Masa watched at first, and then began to stalk. Under cover of a band of thick vegetation she ran fast and low along the riverbank, and hid behind a stand of long grass beside a likely drinking place. Such was her excitement, the tip to her tail twitched uncontrollably.

At first, the wildebeest milled about, none daring to walk down to the water's edge. Instinctively, they knew that the river-side vegetation could be harbouring danger. A family group of zebra, however, were close to the front of the wildebeest herd. The stallion looked carefully at the trees and bushes, and scanned the river for signs of predators. The lioness, though, was well concealed. He could not see her. The stallion began to walk down the embankment. It was a well-worn track, often used by animals walking down to the river to drink. His family followed. Masa let them pass, and seeing that none of the zebra were attacked, the wildebeest began to move too. The lioness readied herself as she searched amongst the tangle of moving legs for signs of a vulnerable calf or juvenile. Spotting one she leaped from her hiding place, but the calf was too quick. It jinked to one side, almost into the path of a bunch of galloping adults, but it kept on running. Masa stood momentarily. She had blown it. The flow of wildebeest stopped immediately. All she could see was a row of wildebeest backsides disappearing over the brow.

By midday, the temperature was soaring and so Masa returned to the cubs and sought out a place where they were shaded by a thick covering of leaves. She would remain there until the temperature dropped, waiting for another chance to ambush anything that came down to drink. The family needed meat. However, although the cubs were eating meat, and increasingly larger quantities of it, they still received a daily supply of milk and would do so until they were anywhere between seven and nine months old. They pummelled their mother's tummy, encouraging the milk to flow and then the two little ones lined up and drank. But the peace would not last for long. While his brother drank, Tatu went exploring on his own. It was something that he would do frequently later in life, much to the chagrin of his brother.

The young lion stopped and stared, and out from behind a bush walked a fully-grown hippo. It was trying to find its way back to the deeper part of the marsh, but the rocky terrain was making it impossible so it was walking along the riverbank looking for a suitable place to drop into the water. Tatu was on the embankment just above him and when the great beast noticed he was there it turned and looked up at him. The youngster sat on his haunches and stared back. He had seen hippos before, but not in the open like this. It seemed even bigger. The hippo, however, was uneasy. It played safe, found a small muddy ramp and eased itself gently into the water. Tatu turned and ran all the way back to mother, fearful that the monster might give chase and catch him. But she had picked up something of more immediate danger.

Masa sniffed the air and pondered what to do. She had picked up the scent of two male lions upwind. They were more nomads from outside the crater, looking for a chance to challenge the resident pride males. But if they found Masa and the two cubs they would surely kill them. She would have little defence against two. Mbili and Tatu had stopped playing and were visibly uncomfortable. The sun was high, the heat intense and there was real danger only tens of metres away. She was desperate to find a hiding place. The lioness looked about her, and made a decision. She led the cubs to a stand of trees and some low bushes and settled down to see what the lions would do. They could not see her, but once they were downwind they could smell her. She watched. If they all survived this, she would move them to a safer place under the cover of darkness.

The two males swaggered off without looking back, but luck was not with this mother today. As the two males were disappearing in one direction, a bachelor herd of buffalo was coming from the other. If they smelled or spotted the cubs they could gore or trample them to death. But this mother was a clever one. She realised she was not far from a hiding place they had used previously – the old fig tree – so she quickly led her cubs to the cub-sized hollow in its base and left them. Then she made herself very conspicuous. She walked back to where the buffalo were pushing through the vegetation. They turned immediately. Now they were only interested in her and what she was doing. As long as she could divert their attention from the fig tree, her cubs would be safe.

At the tree, however, a raucous call announced the appearance of a troop of banded mongooses, the very same group that Masa had met at the rotting log all those months ago. Their log had become so rotten they had had to move and now they were here, in another hollow log next to the fig tree, and they were distinctly nonplussed about sharing it with lions, even if they were cubs. The mongoose family chattered and stared, appeared and disappeared, but the lions were not shifting, so they lined up inside their front door, just their noses poking out. One of the lion cubs went to look, but the mongooses simply withdrew to the back of their log. One brave soul popped up from around the back, but there was no way he was going to venture further afield with Mbili and Tatu outside. They were losing valuable foraging time, but that would have to wait. The lions were showing no signs of going anywhere. And that was the way it was for most of the day – the mongooses trapped in their log and the lion family resting outside.

In the late afternoon, Masa spotted a disturbance. It was a small group of topi and they were heading her way. The mother left her cubs at the fig tree and headed out to the long grass where she could hide.

The topi herd had moved slowly towards the river. They stood on the lip of a low bank, hesitating to go further. Masa spotted the opportunity and went into stalking mode. She crawled, almost flat against the ground, to a spot directly below them, where an overhang hid her. The topi were extremely cautious, looking carefully all around them and sniffing for signs of danger. The lead animal began to walk down the hippo track, while the others gathered at the top of the slope. One by one, they went down, until the entire herd was on the move. The lioness dropped to a crouch, her eyes fixed on the first few animals. Again she searched for the most vulnerable. She waited as increasingly more topi came down to the water's edge and began to drink. She bunched up her muscles, ready to run, but many were still nervous. Some cut short their visit and went back up the slope, while others were still making the descent. The two-way traffic was confusing, but the cat had identified a target, a topi calf. She started to run, hesitated, and then ran again. The topi scattered, the mother and calf making good their escape up a deep gully, leaving Masa behind and face to face with a young topi male who was not running anywhere.

Instead of fleeing with the rest of the herd, he turned on the lioness and it was she who had to run away, not him. He sported a fine set of swept-back horns that would have done considerable damage if he had made contact. Masa had to make sure he did not, but the topi was unbelievably persistent. He chased her back and forth across the grass and she only escaped by rushing into the long grass around the marsh. He was reluctant to enter and so returned to the herd. Masa had had a narrow escape. If she had been injured at all and was unable to hunt, it would have been her cubs who suffered first, not their mother. She had to be careful. They would be dependent on her until they were at least 16 months old, but they were little over four months and still on mother's milk – fifteen minutes of suckling a day – as well as the meat from kills. It had been a sobering experience and she would not forget it in a hurry.

That night Masa broke with traditional. She usually hunted by day to avoid the predators that hunted at night, but despite the prospect of running into hyenas or other lions, she went looking for food, although again she caught nothing. However, during the early morning while she was on her way back to the cubs, she was startled by an ostrich running out at high speed in front of her. It was agitated and certainly panicking. She was tempted to give chase, but with its long and powerful legs it could easily have outrun a lioness. Instead, she sniffed around. Something told her that the bird was hiding something. She took a look at the patch of grass from where the ostrich had appeared. There on the ground was a nest, with 30 or more giant eggs. The ostrich had abandoned it when the lion came close and was now going to regret not defending it. The lioness settled down and broke into the eggs, one by one, licking out their contents and discarding the broken shells. The hair around her mouth and chin turned yellow with the sticky yolk, but at least she had found food that did not run away.

After an hour or so, Masa looked up from her breakfast to find that a herd of wildebeest was crossing a water-filled ditch not far from her. She stood and watched for a moment before crawling, low to the ground as usual, to put herself ahead of the herd. The grass was just high enough to conceal her, so she waited for the animals to come to her. They were in no hurry. They were feeding on patches of green shoots between the stands of longer grass. Even when they came to within a few metres of where the lioness was hiding, they did not know that she was there.

At first, just five or six wildebeest broke off from feeding and went down to the water's edge. Two of them lowered their heads in unison and began to drink. The others milled around. Eventually, they too went to drink. The rest of the herd watched from their safe vantage point, and then, reassured by the advance party, began to move towards the ditch too. Soon, 40 or 50 animals were drinking. Others, however, were eager to cross to the other side. Hidden by thick vegetation, the lioness approached closer. She settled down behind a large bush, the tip of her tail twitching, and waited patiently for the best moment to spring her trap. Row upon row of wildebeest filed past her, but still she did not move. She waited until the last of the herd had gone by and dashed from cover. The wildebeest scattered, but within a few paces Masa brought one down. Such was the precision of her strike, it was all over in seconds. After throttling the beast, she went to find her cubs. It was too early in the day and too cold for vultures to soar, so there was a good chance her family could feed before the scavengers turned up and chased them away.

The family ate quickly. As the temperature rose, thermals were forming high above the crater floor. The first vulture was already in a nearby tree and many others had seen it descend. They would be arriving from all points of the compass and soon there would be a noisy, squabbling group that was sure to attract the attention of scavengers on the ground. Masa looked up as the birds dropped down, then looked around anxiously. This was not good. They had to leave soon, but not before one of the cubs tried to chase the vultures away. They erupted in a mass of flapping wings only to settle back down again a few metres away.

Masa indicated that enough was enough and began to walk away from the kill site. Her cubs followed obediently. She was loath to lose another one. The vultures took over what remained of the carcass. A trio of marabou storks joined them, and they towered over the other birds. And then there was mayhem. The vultures spread their wings, trying to look bigger and more intimidating than they really were. But every bird was trying the same trick, which inevitably ended up as one big squabble. Masa hurried away before hyenas appeared. They were a real danger to her offspring, even though they were not tiny cubs any more.

By the time Mbili and Tatu were five months old, the two brothers were inseparable. They played together constantly and their exploits must have worried their mother sick – that is, if lionesses can be worried sick like human mothers can. Tatu's latest game was stalking zebra. He had no chance of getting near one without being detected and he was still too small to catch anything anyway, but it was all good practice for a time when stalking prey would be a matter of survival. At this stage, Mbili just went along for the ride, but whatever Tatu did always got both of the brothers into trouble. Kicks from an angry zebra could end their lives almost before they had got going, but it did not stop Tatu. He would continue to stalk even though the herd had made it abundantly clear that he had been rumbled.

On one occasion, they got themselves into some real trouble. The two brothers were away from the rest area without their mother when they found themselves in the path of a large herd of grazing buffalo. Tatu was in his element. He had found something big to stalk, and his pretend quarry seemed to be a bunch of peaceful plant-eaters. As a small cub he had been chased and almost trampled to death by these beasts, but for now all that was forgotten – they were little more than playmates . . . and these the most unpredictable and dangerous animals in Africa, well capable of goring or trampling an adult lion, let alone a five-month-old cub. The hostility between lions and buffalo was ongoing, in what amounted to a full-scale war, and both sides regularly took casualties. The brothers were pushing their luck.

Tatu hid behind a line of bushes and crept quietly towards the nearest bull. He lifted his head, licked his nostrils and smelled the air. He had picked up the smell of lion, but he was not sure from where. He licked his nose again, the moisture gathering more odours for his brain to analyse. He snorted. Other buffalo looked up. They stopped grazing. They had all caught the scent.

The old bull swung his head from side to side and advanced towards the place where the two young lions were hiding. Tatu realised the danger they were in and fled, Mbili close behind. They ran as fast as they could, using a line of bushes to cover their escape. But the buffalo were still coming. They were tracking the cubs by following their scent, and they had started to run. Tatu looked around nervously. The entire herd was heading their way.

Tatu ran, leaving Mbili behind. In seconds the buffalo were upon him. The frightened cub crawled into a ditch and cowered beneath an overhanging clod of earth. The buffalo could not see him but they could certainly smell him. A moving wall of horns and hooves surrounded him

Suddenly Masa appeared. She ran in front of the leading buffalo, distracting it away from Mbili. She ducked and squirmed, avoiding the formidable horns, and slowly diverted the herd into chasing her. She had really put her life on the line, but it worked. She led them to a thicket, disappearing through a gap and reappearing on the other side. The buffalo descended on the dense vegetation, thrashing and trampling, but all to no avail. Masa had already gone.

Looking rather sheepish, Tatu ran up to his mother, hoping for a reassuring greeting, but all he got was a cuff against his ear, just as any naughty boy might receive. Mbili, however, was still missing. Masa, with Tatu in tow, walked in a great arc to avoid the buffalo, and returned to the place where the attack had started. She called. It was a muffled sound, not loud enough to alert the herd or any lions but sufficient to summon the cub . . . if he was still alive.

There was no answer and no cub. Either Mbili was dead or he was too frightened to come out. Masa and Tatu continued their search, combing every centimetre of the place. Still nothing. Then, there was an audible bleat. Mbili appeared from behind a rock. Emerging from his hiding place he ran first to Tatu. His mother licked the top of his head. And that was that. They had survived another of Tatu's great adventures. The three of them returned to their resting site, while over at the thicket the buffalo were still trashing the place and would be doing so for a good while longer. The brothers had had a very narrow escape.

That evening, the plains came alive with vibrant colour. With the sun low on the western horizon, the entire place was bathed in a golden glow. Wherever the ground had dried out, there were clouds of terra cotta dust that betrayed animals on the move. They had crisp, dark outlines and their long shadows stretched away to create a mosaic of changing shapes on the ground. A flock of red-billed quelea, thought to be the most numerous bird on Earth, fell on a great expanse of long grass that was setting seed. There must have been hundreds of thousands of birds present. They chattered and screamed, the noise deafening, but when a jackal spooked them, they took to the air in a confusion of tiny bodies and vibrating wings. The huge, amorphous flock swirled like a giant amoeba, its dark, constantly changing shape dominated the cloudless sky. Each bird was no bigger than a sparrow, yet in these numbers they could devastate a crop, bringing famine to places where hunger was never far away.

At the end of their first year, the brothers were showing distinct signs of adolescence. They were almost as big as their mother, and the first tufts of a rather scruffy mane were beginning to appear around their face and neck. They still came to greet Masa, rubbing heads enthusiastically. They still depended on her for food, in fact, they sometimes tried to suckle, but Masa's milk was drying up and increasingly they were joining in with the hunt.

It was then that the brothers took their next significant step in life. Along with Masa, they had been wandering far and wide, when they came to a long stretch of riverine forest. They had to go carefully, as this was the heart of the Lakeside Pride's territory, the place where their lionesses came to give birth, and a favourite place to rest up. It was a dangerous place to be, but the coast was clear.

One of the brothers was suddenly alert, staring intently at something ahead. The other came up and joined him and was looking too. They had spotted a topi mother and her calf, but instead of holding back and waiting for mother, the impulsive Tatu went into stalking mode and moved quickly towards the calf with intention of making a kill. He started to run, but the target calf was already up and running, and quickly out-paced the young lion. However, as he stopped, Mbili took over. Like a runner in a relay race, he continued the chase and sprinted after the calf. The two brothers, though, did not have the same turn of speed as their mother. She could reach close to 80 kph in just three seconds, and run at that speed for 300–400 metres. They had to give up, but this was their first real hunt, a milestone in their lives.

The exhilaration of the chase, however, was tempered by its aftermath – they had attracted too much attention. All the topi and several small herds of Thomson's gazelle began to crowd around the two brothers. They might have been small antelope but they were actually mobbing the two young cats. They were demonstrating that Mbili and Tatu had been spotted, and therefore the young lions had no chance of catching one of them now. As the crowd of gazelles and antelope edged gradually closer, a topi mother stepped out of the crowd, and walked menacingly towards the brothers. They turned and ran, high-tailing it back to mother, but they were not chastened. Their next attempt was even more ambitious.

Masa was out alone. She had tried to make contact with the pride, but again Hasimu thwarted any hope of reconciliation. The pride males had been receptive to her, but Hasimu had ensured that the other lionesses ganged up against her. She had avoided a fight, so she was in one piece. She plodded back to the last place she had left her two adolescents. They, however, were out on their second hunting excursion without her. They were starting to behave like grown-up cats, except that on this foray they began to stalk three giraffes, unlikely prey for two delinquent lions. Their 'quarry' looked down disdainfully at the young predators. Tatu charged but, to add insult to injury, the giraffes stood stock-still and just stared at the young upstart. Both he and Mbili retreated to the bushes, before heading back down to the river. On the way, their inexperience showed yet again. This time, the chosen target was no less than a young hippo – not the easiest animal to subdue, no matter its size. It may have been a juvenile, but it was still one of the most powerful animals in the marsh.

As the young lions approached, it promptly put its rear end against the floor to protect it, leaving its gigantic mouth to chomp at its attackers. They wisely kept clear of the head end, and focussed their attack on the other end, even though it was out of reach. The skin on the hippo's back was remarkably thick so their teeth and claws could get little purchase. Tatu jumped on to its back but simply slipped off. This galvanised the hippo into moving. It swivelled its body around so that its head end confronted the two lions. They jumped back almost as one. The hippo stood up and started to walk back to the river. They tried to bite at its rump and jumped on and off its back, but it just kept on walking. Then it stopped and sat on its backside again. Mbili and Tatu lunged at the beast, but still their assault was having little effect. The hippo rose again and sought refuge in the bushes at the top of the riverbank. Only metres from the safety of the water, he sat again, but suddenly the two brothers stopped their attack and made off. The confused hippo sat for a while. His attackers had simply evaporated and, apart from a few gashes, he was still in one piece. He followed a track down the bank and into the river. It was then that he realised why his assailants had left in a hurry. There were people with livestock down at the water's edge. Mbili and Tatu had already learned about them.

Jumping from one slab of rock to the next near the water's edge was Masa. She was heading upstream, to where Mbili and Tatu were waiting. They were big boys now. All three rubbed heads and sauntered together along the riverbank. The brothers were almost adult-size and noticeably larger than their mother, yet they still sponged on her for food. They would soon be ready for independence but, for the moment, they were still mother's boys. Nevertheless, they were doing many more grown-up things. Every few metres, they brushed through the vegetation and began to scent mark, and they even tried a few roars, although they were quick to move location lest the pride males find them. It was becoming increasingly dangerous for them to remain in the crater. More prides had formed or reformed after the great plague, so there were more fully mature males about. The Lakeside Pride was hemmed in by several other prides, but they were strong. For the moment they had nothing to fear from the new neighbours. It did mean, however, that Masa and her boys had to hunt increasingly away from the river, and it was on the open grassland that they were to make the next step to adulthood.

Mbili and Tatu flanked Masa, and the three of them were making for a line of trees that would lead them straight into the middle of a large, mixed herd of wildebeest and zebra. They walked out in the open at first, for all to see, the boys strutting and their mother walking nonchalantly. But when they reached cover, they were almost invisible. They split up, Mbili going to the left and Tatu to the right. The wildebeest were feeding or standing peacefully, but then suddenly one group started to stampede. Others followed until the entire herd was galloping. When the dust settled, the cause was evident. There was Mbili with a wildebeest calf held by the throat and he was throttling the life out of it. It was his first solo kill, but now he had to keep it.

The lion family were some distance from cover by now, so Mbili straddled the carcass as he had seen his mother do and dragged it towards some low bushes. He stopped and caught his breath, looked around for any signs of hyenas or other lions, and then picked it up again by the neck and dragged it some more. He moved with surprising speed, stopping every few metres to look around. When he reached the place where he could hide the body, Masa and Tatu joined him. They rubbed heads and bodies in greeting. Mbili had done well. It was only a calf but it would do. They tucked in, but Tatu snarled and seized the largest portion. He disappeared into the thicket, leaving his mother and brother with very little. Tatu was already playing the role of pride male – letting the others do the hard work and then taking over the kill, but it would be a very long time before he had a pride of his own.

Not long after their second birthday, it was time for the boys to leave. They had learned well how to be lions, learned well the ways of the savannah. Their mother had taught them that. They were killers, but they were killers with a purpose. Lions and the other predators in the crater ensured that the weaker members of the community were excised from the population and the fit survived, so the community remained healthy. But they were about to leave that community. There was no place for them in the crater any more.

Masa snarled at her two sons. It was a painful thing to do, but she had to force them to go. If they stayed they would always be hounded and even killed by the pride males. Their only way was to leave the crater, as many young lions had done before them. They rubbed heads with their mother for one last time, but then she chased them away.

They walked up the elephant track that led out of the crater. Mbili turned. His mother stared, and then the two brothers continued up the slope. They paused again, but as they turned to look back, they saw Hasimu and the rest of the Lakeside Pride heading towards Masa. Without warning, their mother attacked Hasimu. She was ruthless, gouging out great chunks of fur and slashing at Hasimu's face. They rose up on their hind legs and crashed to the ground, but Masa was up first and tore into Hasimu's rump, causing deep and bloody gashes to appear through her coat. Hasimu's legs buckled and she rolled on to her back. She tucked up her legs to protect her belly, but Masa was quick. She grabbed Hasimu by the throat and this time she would not let go. Within minutes, Hasimu was dead. The pride did not move. They simply stared. Masa lay panting beside Hasimu's inert body. The young lioness had had her revenge.

The dark-maned lion walked towards her, the others in the pride not far behind, but instead of attacking they all stopped. The lion rubbed heads with Masa, then walked away. Masa followed. The lakeside lionesses crowded around and rubbed heads too. She had been accepted by the pride. She would be a single mother no more. The brothers watched from high on the crater wall. They turned to go. Now they had to find their own way in the world. Now they had to be real lions.

CHAPTER FOUR

– Two Brothers –

When Mbili and Tatu reached the rim of the crater it was early morning. They had camped out on the crater wall, not far from the place where they were born, before pressing on at first light, but all they could see was thick cloud. The fog enveloped them, almost choked them. They could barely see a few metres ahead. It was a little scary, not knowing what was around them and more importantly what might be close by. They felt more than a little vulnerable in this strange place and were in two minds whether to turn on their heels and go back down the track, and back into the crater where they would be surrounded once again by everything that was familiar. But they had no choice. They rubbed heads, paused for breath, and walked on.

An exquisite golden-winged sunbird flew out from the mountain forest, startling the two young lions. It hovered by a cluster of flowers, where several more birds joined in. Then, some more arrived and a fight broke out. The feathers were flying. The first group were all close relatives who were defending this patch from the intruders. It was their way of making sure their cupboard was well stocked. By guarding their flowers, valuable nectar – their fuel supply – accumulated during the day and was undisturbed by other nectar feeders. Mbili stared as they fluttered about, and then they were gone just as suddenly as they had arrived, when out of the mist, the ominous shape of a bull elephant appeared. With little wind, he had failed to pick up the lions' scent, and he was as startled to see the young lions as they were of seeing him. He trumpeted a warning. He was on his way to the crater for a little relaxation and recovery, and was not at all interested in chasing a couple of cats. Nevertheless, Mbili and Tatu gave him a wide berth.

After an hour of clambering through gullies etched by thousands of years of heavy rains and over ridges of black volcanic rocks, they felt the ground beneath them beginning to drop. They were heading downhill and the long trek down the steep outer slopes of the extinct volcano to the plains below. Visibility was still poor, but improving. The sun was burning through the fog and it was starting to clear and, as they reached the lower slopes, the two brothers were able to see the plains for the very first time . . . and what a sight it was.

They had been used to a world where the steep walls of the crater were all they could see in the distance. It had been their fortress, but it was also their prison, and now they had broken out, and the landscape they saw before them was very different. There was rolling grassland as far as the eye could see, but even more enticing was the extraordinary abundance of food, and it was right there in front of them. All they had to do was to go and take it. The plains were packed with wildebeest – millions of them, the herds stretching from one horizon to the other. Walking amongst them were parties of zebra, conspicuous in their black-and-white stripes, as well as gangs of Thomson's and Grant's gazelles, impala, and a solitary hartebeest. A topi, perched on an old termite mound, was the sentinel for his small herd of cows and calves, and standing taller and more imposing than the rest was an eland, as big as a prize ox and with spiral horns to match. In the distance, a herd of elephants, with cows and calves of all sizes, were led by an enormous matriarch, not far from a rhino mother and her docile calf. By a watercourse, a herd of buffalo wallowed in the mud alongside a family of warthogs. Mbili and Tatu could not believe their eyes. It was a lion's paradise. Never had they seen so many animals in one place.

It was January and the animals had been on the short grass plains for a month or so. The short rains had fallen during November and December and the grass was still lush and full of the minerals that would be vital for producing milk when the wildebeest have their calves in a few weeks' time. For now, the scattered herds were grazing. Occasionally, a group would stampede, spooked by some unseen danger, putting clouds of cattle egrets to flight. But with nearly one-and-a-half million wildebeest and a quarter-of-a-million zebra before them, where should they start? The two brothers were overwhelmed. They lay down and just stared.

As they rested on the side of the hill, there was a sudden, deep, reverberating roar. Both of them snapped out of their daze, leaped up and dived for cover. One of the local pride males had let them know whose territory they had entered and he was not happy to have two young delinquents in his kingdom. He roared again, and they went straight through, rather than around, a thick bush and came out the other side, their scraggy manes covered with twigs and dead leaves. They were bounding as fast as they dare down the steep slope, ending up in an acacia thicket where they hid until the lion ceased its roaring.

After waiting for what seemed an eternity, the two brothers plucked up courage to emerge from the bush. Mbili walked out first, but Tatu was not following. Mbili turned to look for his brother, and saw that Tatu had a thorn twig stuck into his nose and he could not move. He was impaled. His eyes watered copiously. Mbili took a closer look, licked the wound, but Tatu was firmly caught. Each time he moved it was excruciatingly painful. Then, Mbili did a most extraordinary thing . . . at least for a lion. He was actually trying to get it out. He lifted his paw and hit the twig, and then licked again the place where the thorn was digging in. He did it again and again, each time attempting to dislodge the thorny twig. Try as he might, though, Tatu could not get free at first, but then he simply twisted his head and the thorn came out. He licked his nose, shook his head and walked on as if nothing had happened. Mbili came up alongside. They rubbed heads and shoulders, and then walked on together.

They had not eaten since the day before yesterday, and that had been a relatively small meal of baby warthog. They were hungry. They looked around them, at all the game. It was still there. The bout of roaring had nothing to do with the wildebeest, zebra and gazelles so they continued to graze. Surely the brothers could catch something here, but their aspirations were far bigger than their capabilities. They began with something that stood out from the crowd, none other than a bull eland, a giant of an antelope. They had seen eland in the crater, but this was an enormous beast. All that meat must have been just too enticing, but they had not taken account of the horns, and the powerful animal beneath them.

The eland stood over one-and-a-half metres at the shoulder, his dark tan coat indicating a mature animal. His horns were tight spirals, about 50 centimetres long, his neck was massive, and he had a distinct dewlap under his chin. He was in his prime. The brothers could not have chosen a more formidable beast, but they were not to be put off. They zigzagged back and forth in the long grass in front of him, trying to confuse him, but he was having none of it. He lowered his head and charged first Tatu and then Mbili. Both lions had to leap clear or they would have been skewered. They ran. That was one species they would not stalk again in a hurry.

The eland did not press home his attack, so the boys laid down to rest once more. All this racing about and trying to catch things was hard work, and they were drawing attention to themselves in a place where they were definitely not welcome. They had to be more careful. This time, in true lion fashion, they would wait and see what came to them. And they waited . . . and waited . . . and waited . . . but they were so conspicuous, even with their adolescent haircuts, nothing came within a half a kilometre of them.

And so it went on for the rest of the day, failed hunt following failed hunt. Independence had certainly come as something of a shock to the two brothers, but it was still a charming time in their lives. Sometimes they were kitten-like; other times they had to behave as their mother had taught them. With bags of energy, they still had time to play, rough-and-tumble, biting and fighting, slapping and snapping, but they had always to be alert for the unexpected.

Their play fighting came to an abrupt halt when they disturbed a snake – a spitting cobra. Tatu was about to attack when it reared up. It spread its dark hood, making it seem even more formidable than it already was. Tatu jumped back, which was just as well. This was a dangerous snake. It could eject venom, like a water pistol, and should it get into a lion's eyes it would be blinded immediately. But hot headed as usual, Tatu was about to attack again when fear fortunately got the better of him. Mbili was more circumspect, circling the snake, snarling at it. The snake was erect and ready to strike. Tatu became impatient and lunged forward. Without warning the snake spat, a gob of venom splattering on to Tatu's face, a minute drop getting into his eye. He raised his paw to rub it and blinked uncontrollably. His eye was burning and watering profusely, and for the moment he could not see properly. The snake slunk away. The lions did not follow. They were learning something new almost every moment of every day, and sometimes, like today, it was not a pleasant experience at all.

While the injured Tatu sat on the sidelines, Mbili switched from play to serious hunting. It was time to catch their first meal and, right on cue, a herd of wildebeest and zebra had moved and were milling about in front of them. Mbili trotted out, spooking the wildebeest. They began to run. The panic was infectious, causing increasingly more to start to move until they had a full-blown stampede. How was he to pin down something in this chaos?

Mbili continued to move around, not hurrying but keeping an eye open for an animal that might make a mistake and blunder into them. It never came, and so both predator and prey began to settle down. He flopped down beside his brother, while the wildebeest went back to grazing, but careful to be well clear of the two unpredictable lions.

After a short while, Tatu became bored. Despite his painful eye, he got up and walked straight into the middle of the herd. The small groups close to him panicked and ran. He watched carefully with his good eye for signs of a calf or a juvenile, something which they could tackle without too much trouble. Wildebeest were running back and forth, but still there was nothing. He speeded up to a trot, moving parallel to a group of adults. But they were galloping past him. There was no way he was going to knock over any of them. He stood in the middle of the pandemonium, frustrated that none would fall over for him – the king of beasts. He was a lion, after all!

As the light was failing at the end of the day, Mbili and Tatu tried one more time. They would look again for a calf or a youngster that was not too big or would not run too fast, although they had failed to notice that, at that time, there were no calves on the plains. Wildebeest births were not for several weeks, in February, but it did not stop them looking. Again they tried the scare-and-scatter tactic. They ran right in amongst the wildebeest, so that animals were galloping all around them. They were searching for that vulnerable calf but all they could see were adults, and all males at that. They had inadvertently barged into a bachelor herd; there would never be any calves in there.

They were quickly surrounded, and Mbili became separated from Tatu. The wildebeest realised that he was alone and vulnerable, so instead of the lion chasing them, they began to chase him. The bachelors lined up and advanced in line abreast, a formidable wall of black faces and sharp, upturned horns. They were mobbing Mbili and were quite unafraid. He searched for his brother, spotted him on the other side of a thicket and ran. The two cats had learned another lesson – wildebeest are not necessarily as docile as they look – but still they had not fed.

The brothers were noticeably thin. Their flanks were drawn in, their coat lacked lustre and they were generally looking gaunt. If they did not eat soon, they would be in real trouble for they would not be able to move, let alone hunt. A lone hartebeest was the next in line. Mbili crawled directly toward the prey, while Tatu went out to the right, trying to outflank it. Mbili tried to make himself as flat as he possibly could. Just the black tips to his ears showed above the grass, but the hartebeest had already spotted them. It was uneasy. It stamped its forefoot to the ground and fled. Mbili could only look on. Tatu came to join him. They cuffed each other playfully and then rolled in the grass, disturbing a Thomson's gazelle fawn that had been hiding there. If was off in an instant, before the brothers could even get to their feet. Tatu gave chase, but it was no good. The fawn disappeared into the distance . . . two sitting ducks, and two misses. The brothers were not doing very well at all.

By sunset, they had had several more opportunities and several more failures. It was with desperation they picked up the unmistakable odour of a recently opened body cavity – probably a carcass of some sort – and followed it back to its source. If the predators involved were small or weak enough, perhaps they could muscle in on the kill and steal it for themselves. But as they came over the top of a rise they realised they had walked straight into a lioness and two lions from the local pride. They were feasting on their kill and failed to notice the two brothers.

Mbili and Tatu backed away slowly, and hid amongst the croton bushes. From here they could watch the lions and not be seen. There was the faintest chance that there would be leftovers, normally a snack for hyenas, which eat just about anything – bones, hair, guts and all. By now, though, the brothers would settle for any morsel, no matter how small.

They had to wait, though. It was a couple of hours before the lions left, so under cover of darkness, first Mbili and then Tatu crept out of their hiding place and down to the remains of the carcass. It was, indeed, bereft of meat. The pride had done a thorough job of stripping it almost clean, but there were a few fragments clinging to the bone, and a pile of intestines had been left. Tatu scoffed the entrails and took the head and gnawed at the cheeks, while Mbili chewed whatever he could from the rest of the bones. After a couple of hours, little was left. They had licked the skeleton clean. The brothers went back to their croton bush and lay down until just before sunrise.

It was a perfect dawn, the sun a great, red orb rising into a pale blue sky accompanied by wispy clouds edged in red, yellow and gold. Screeching hornbills vied with bustards and spurfowl to dominate the dawn chorus, and the frozen silhouette of a topi, standing alert on a termite mound, was the only indication that the brothers were up and about. They passed a pair of secretary birds, treading with determination in their search for insects and even snakes in the grass. An elephant threw dust over its back and disappeared momentarily inside a terracotta cloud. At a waterhole, buffalo had waded into the water up to their bellies, the spray causing the oxpeckers that had been riding on their backs to scatter in alarm. But they soon returned to cleaning duties, hanging on to the buffaloes' ears and muzzles, picking off parasites and dead skin. The brothers walked on, searching for the slightest hint of prey that they could actually bring down or even scavenge from another predator.

And this was the way it went for several more days. They walked and walked and, although they were surrounded by an abundance of game, they just could not catch anything. Then, one morning they came to a small river, more a stream than a river, but it was clearly a magnet for thirsty animals, and there just ahead of them was a small herd of impala milling about close to the water.

They were the perfect antelope – sleek, long-legged and proud. A male stood erect, his S-curved horns held aloft to show to all that this was his territory, at least for a few months. Gathered about him were a bevy of females, their two-tone brown coats glistening with dew. The two lions lowered their bodies to the ground and began to stalk. Their eyes did not move from the group. Other impala some distance away gave the sneezing alarm call. They had seen the lions, but the group by the water could not see what the alarm was about. They were nervous, as impala tend to be normally, but continued to drink. Every so often they lifted their heads abruptly, staring about them and twisting their ears, searching for any signs of danger, before lowering again. An impala with its head down was only a few metres from Mbili. He started his run. The impala took off. It leaped nearly three metres into the air. Mbili pulled up quickly. He could not believe his eyes. He just stood and stared as his quarry escaped. It bounced rather than ran away into the distance, leaving the young lion puzzled that he could have lost a meal that was so close.

His sibling walked over to greet him and, as usual, they rubbed heads before heading down to the river. The vegetation here was dense, giving the lions cover from which to launch their attacks, but there was also the pervading scent of lions all around. This was a favourite hunting place for the resident pride. They had left their smell behind, but for the moment they were elsewhere in their territory. Mbili and Tatu made themselves at home.

A party of cisticolas – members of the warbler family – chattered from the bushes and trees by the water, and a plover rooted about in the mud at the water's edge. Flycatchers darted in and out of the vegetation, catching insects, and an eagle swooped overhead, a cane rat in its sights. Upstream, an elephant sucked up water in its trunk and squirted it over his back. Several others stood around, their trunks raised, testing the air for any sign of danger. One young elephant playfully pulled another's tail and they plodded away into the distance. Tranquillity . . . but still no food.

The young lions moved cautiously to the water. First one,

and then the other began to drink. They lapped just like domestic cats, but checking constantly over their shoulders should anything creep up behind them. They were on an exposed beach and highly vulnerable if the local pride should come along. Their thirst slaked, they jumped over at the narrowest crossing point and disappeared into the thick vegetation on the other side, the territory of the neighbouring pride.

Within a few minutes Mbili pulled up short. He was separated from Tatu by some bushes, so Tatu had not seen Mbili stop, and directly ahead of them was a lioness sitting on her haunches. She was one of the locals, and where there was one there could be more, so Mbili took evasive action. He circled quickly around the other side of a thicket, checking constantly that the lioness was not following. Tatu, however, was hidden from the lioness by the bush. He did not know that she was there, so when he came into the open, they were face to face. He did not wait for any response but walked away as nonchalantly as possible, adopting an almost sideways motion . . . and then, he left the area . . . rapidly.

Having crossed to the other side, the lions moved away from the river. They trekked for several hours without any chance of running down a meal, but they were heading unwittingly into pastoral land. All around them were small herds of cattle and other domestic stock, and keeping their eye on their animals were the herdsmen. The brothers had already learned from their run-in at the crater that herdsmen should be avoided at all costs, but here was food aplenty and the animals seemed to be sitting ducks. In the main, the herdsmen kept their herds away and therefore safe from the natural predators, but these young lions were going straight into their domain. If Mbili or Tatu should as much as touch a cow, sheep or goat, they would both be in grave danger. Such was the importance of a herdsman's livestock, he would spear anything or anybody that should do them harm. The lions were in a difficult but also tantalising situation.

They watched as the procession of cattle passed by. They were being taken back to the corral for the night, but the lions had spotted a calf. They moved forward, oblivious to the presence of the herdsmen and the danger they posed. The promise of easy meat was almost too strong, but at the last moment they saw the people and the spears, and the memory came flooding back. They left the area quickly and returned to the bush.

The following morning they walked the boundary, farmlands on one side, wilderness on the other, and so far they had kept out of trouble. Then, they turned and headed back on to the plains. The natural game was still a sufficient draw to pull them away from the domestic herds. At the sight of three impala, all with their heads down and feeding, Mbili and Tatu began to stalk once more. They had to cross some open ground to get to them, however, which meant if they were spotted they would have to run far and fast. The odds were in the impalas' favour.

Nevertheless, the lions closed the gap without being spotted. Using whatever cover was available, they managed to approach to within 20 metres of their quarry, but it was still a long way if the impala should bolt. The two brothers were together. Mbili started to run and got to within ten metres before the impala burst into life. The young lion accelerated rapidly, reached his top speed and overtook his target before it had really got going. He grabbed one of its back legs, while Tatu came alongside and grabbed the animal's throat. Within a few seconds it toppled, and in a few minutes it was dead. The young lions had something substantial to eat at last.

By February, things began to look up. Many of the wildebeest were agitated and milling around aimlessly. It was time for the females to give birth, and they would all do so within a two- to three-week window. The strategy was sound, if somewhat cruel. Some youngsters would be giving up their life for the greater cause. If every wildebeest mother gave birth at the same time, the predators could not eat all the young, so the majority survive at the expense of a few. The brothers were about to experience a food bonanza, and easy to catch food at that, but for the moment they were unaware that things were changing in their favour.

They had placed themselves on a small rise, so they could see some distance over the plains. From here they could spot something interesting to eat or something that could be a threat, and the first sign that circumstances were changing was when Mbili spotted a female cheetah in the middle distance. The smaller cat just exuded speed, even when she was strolling. Her long, muscular legs, lean body and small head were built for rapid acceleration and a short, sharp pursuit . . . but she was delicate. Like a thoroughbred racehorse, the cheetah's natural design was on the edge of what was possible, which made her highly vulnerable in the kill-or-be-killed environment of the East African savannah.

Mbili watched as the cheetah began to stalk. His ears pricked up and he was ready to act. If the smaller cat caught anything, the brothers could easily steal it. The cheetah, meanwhile, had approached as close as she dare to a herd of wildebeest. They were filing past, and several had already seen her, but ignored her. A cheetah is no threat to an adult wildebeest, but it was not an adult she was stalking. She had a newborn calf in her sights. She waited patiently for it to come close, and then she ran. The chase was brief. The cheetah slammed into the side of the calf, grabbing its throat in the process. It fell. The cat tried keep its grip, but immediately was forced to let go as the calf's mother raced in for the rescue. The cheetah bolted. She was no match for this angry mother. The calf got to its feet and followed its mother back to the herd.

Mbili was on his feet. This was something they had to try for themselves. Tatu came up beside him. They scanned the plains, looking for female wildebeest either lying down or standing still for an unusual amount of time, but they saw nothing. Mbili decided to take a closer look.

The two lions moved in harmony. They were brothers, after all. They were out hunting wildebeest calves and they would work out their own way of catching them. Instead of hiding and stalking, they trotted right up to the herd in full view. Each animal turned to face the two cats. They were ready for an attack, but none came. Instead, the young lions suddenly accelerated and ran right into the midst of the herd, causing instant panic. The wildebeest scattered in all directions, while the two lions looked out for any calves that might be hidden behind the moving wall of legs. It was a tactic that should have worked, but on this occasion there were none. In their rush to take advantage of this new food source, again the two of them had run in amongst a bachelor herd of adult males. All they could do was to retreat as gracefully and as quickly as they could.

At this time of year, more than any other, wildebeest society was highly structured. Nursery groups comprising of cows with calves were separated from mothers about to give birth, while one-year-old calves that had recently left their mothers formed a group of their own, and there were bachelor herds, which kept themselves to themselves and were chased away from the birthing grounds by the older, more dominant males. Mbili and Tatu had run inadvertently into the wrong kind of herd, and they were lucky not to be injured, for the male wildebeest could have been aggressive and attacked the young lions. They had to wander around looking for the right sort of herd, and the location of the birthing grounds themselves.

After a few hours, they found a herd with calves, but they all looked very spritely and well capable of outrunning the two lions. And there were no females giving birth. They were too late. It had occurred in the early morning, and very few wildebeest gave birth after midday. The brothers had to wait.

However, all this activity was attracting other lions as well as clans of hyenas, and the brothers were no match for either at this time. They tried to conceal themselves as best as they could, but there was little cover except for a couple of trees on a small hill. They made for them and camped out in their shade. From here they could see in all directions. In the daytime heat, though, the larger predators would sure to be resting, so the brothers should have been able to relax. They had not reckoned on the local pride, though, and they were little over a half-kilometre away, walking through and hidden by a natural drainage ditch. Lying underneath the trees, Mbili and Tatu could not see them, but after a few minutes Mbili caught their scent on the wind. He rose carefully, lest he be seen and quietly withdrew. Tatu caught on immediately and knew something was amiss. The locals were out hunting and heading their way.

Tatu was about to turn and roar, but thought better of it. It was not the time for any kind of bravado. The brothers trotted away, keeping clear of the resident pride. They found another hillock topped with boulders, and hid there for the rest of the day. The plains below were littered with wildebeest and calves, but they dare not go out while the others were hunting. They had to bide their time. Mbili watched enviously as predators and scavengers converged on the birthing grounds, and next to appear was a pack of wild dogs.

Mbili had once seen them hunting in the crater, but they were no longer there. They were locally extinct. However, this pack on the plains was doing well, and they took full advantage of the glut of food. They timed their own breeding season to that of the wildebeest. Rearing cubs when food was plentiful was a successful survival strategy, and the size of this pack bore this out. There were seven adults and sub-adults, led by the alpha pair. For most of the year they survived on gazelles, scouring a home range of more than 1,500 square kilometres for their prey, but when the wildebeest arrived they switched to calves, and they were right on their doorstep.

The pack left their den and their 12 puppies at sun-up. Trotting in a line, they went out on to the plain and homed in on their first victim. At some hidden signal they began to spread out and they all started to run. The wildebeest scattered, but they already had a target and would pursue it until they caught it. African wild dogs are not sprinters but long-distance runners. Nevertheless, they raced at speeds of up to 60kph during the chase, and could have kept going for over five kilometres at just under 50kph if they had to.

Mbili watched as they singled out a mother with calf, separating them from the rest of the herd. They ran with their white-tipped tails erect and their ears flat against their heads. They called continuously as they nipped at the heels of the prey, then with consummate skill they separated the calf from its mother. She was held at bay by two of the dogs, while the others brought down her offspring. They killed by disembowelling, and within a minute they were all feeding voraciously. It was all over, from beginning to end, in just ten minutes. And when they finished that meal they went off in search of another, carefully to avoid the local lions, but still averaging two kills a day during the birthing season.

As they left, Mbili noticed they had left the head and backbone of the wildebeest calf. Keeping low to the ground, lest he be seen, he ran to collect the remains and brought them back to their refuge. Tatu had the head and Mbili the rest. Again, they gnawed on the bones. It was cold comfort for the so-called kings of the jungle.

At dusk, Mbili and Tatu ventured out of their refuge and scoured the countryside for suitable prey, but found themselves playing cat and mouse with the pride. Each time they started to stalk, the pride lionesses or a bunch of hyenas came along and took their quarry from almost under their noses. It was a frustrating night. Eventually, exhausted and hungry they returned to their hiding place and slept for the rest of the night. The following morning they returned to the wildebeest birthing grounds.

With no sign of the local pride, Mbili and Tatu focussed all their attention on what was going on in front of them. They watched for any signs of females ready to drop their calves. If they were lucky they could catch both mother and unborn calf, an exceptional feast. And then they saw a potential target – a wildebeest whose back legs sparkled in the low morning sun because her waters had broken. She flopped on to the ground, the tips of the hooves of her offspring clearly visible. She was about to give birth.

Mbili and Tatu kept as low as they could and stalked their quarry. They were coming with the sun behind them, so the rest of the herd had difficulty in seeing them. They were just about to start their run when a zebra stallion whinnied his alarm. The wildebeest giving birth was instantly on her feet, and running. Despite being in labour, she ran and fast. She had been saved by an ability to arrest the birthing process when danger threatens. The lions just stood and watched her go. Even in her present state she had the speed and stamina to outdistance them. The rest of the herd, however, looked in the direction of the two exasperated lions. They had been rumbled. There would be no more surprise attacks that morning. It seemed running down wildebeest calves and pregnant mothers was much harder than it first appeared. The brothers flopped down and waited for another chance.

With the rest of the herd on full alert, many other wildebeest mothers took the opportunity to give birth without too much fear of being interrupted. As their contractions increased some stood while others lay on their sides. Mbili watched as one mother was flat on her side, her face contorted and her teeth exposed with the effort. Her baby's head appeared. If the lions should attack now, she had reached the point of no return. Labour could not be interrupted now, but the brothers were unaware of that.

The female lay on the ground and pushed. Part of the calf's slim body emerged, but as she stood up, gravity took over. The baby fell in a heap on the ground, breaking the umbilical cord. She turned and began to lick her newborn – a boy – eating some of the membrane in order to release the little one inside. His gangly legs twitched, and then he began to move. Within a couple of minutes, he was trying to get to his feet, first sitting and then standing, the amniotic sac draped over his shoulders like an overcoat. He tottered but immediately fell back and rolled over backwards, only to try all over again. It was not long before he was propped up on all fours, and he began to take his first steps.

Other females began to gather around. They sniffed the newborn, and went away to give birth themselves. The calf was still a little unsteady and fell again, but within seconds his back legs were splayed and, using his front legs to push his chin from the ground, he was on all fours again. He wobbled to his mother and took his first drink of milk. He was just five minutes old. There would be many more births that morning, each one the same little miracle, and within half-an-hour of being born the calves would be running and prancing like spring lambs, well able to keep up with the herd. During just three weeks over a half-a-million calves would be born – a boom time for carnivores.

By late morning the brothers had had enough of watching and were intent on doing. When they went out on to the plains, there were a few wildebeest mothers still in labour. They walked brazenly towards the herd. They spotted one that had lain down. They would try the same tactic again – scattering the herd, and grab something in the confusion. However, this time it worked . . . up to a point. The calf was on its feet and, far from being the spindly, wobbly baby that the brothers had expected, it was already able to run. It took flight but could barely keep up with its mother. In a week or so, it would be able to run as fast as the adults and outrun any predators, but for now it somehow had to survive this day.

Suddenly, Mbili stopped. A group of hyenas ran into the herd. They quickly placed themselves alongside one of the mothers and were snapping at her calf. She stopped and bent her head to ram one of them with her horns. It sidestepped and she missed, but the hyena continued to engage with the mother, harassing her continuously. And while she was preoccupied with two hyenas, the others grabbed the calf. It was dead with a single bite to the head. The mother tried to gore the hyenas but they evaded her horns easily, and then they ganged up on her and drove her away. After a short tussle over who was to have what, the hyenas tore into the calf's body ripping it apart, and then they ran off, each with its choice cut. But the sideshow had saved the other calf's life. It disappeared into the distance alongside its mother. Mbili and Tatu looked on forlornly. It was tough being a lion.

The brothers were failing again, but their luck was about to change, and in an unexpected way. Walking straight towards them was another wildebeest calf. During the stampede it had become separated from its mother. It was bleating loudly, searching everywhere. Other females with calves, and even those without, had sniffed it and rejected it. It had been passed from one to the next, until there came a point when it would approach any large animal – elephants, rhinos . . . and even lions. Tatu saw the orphan and instinctively tried to make himself as inconspicuous as possible by flattening his body to the ground. The calf was not duped, but that was its undoing. As it tottered up to Tatu, thinking he could be its mother, the lion pounced and killed it with a single bite. Mbili trotted over. He could not believe it had been so easy.

The young lions, though, were clearly visible from many kilometres away. Their kill was sure to attract attention. Vultures and eagles were constantly circling the birthing ground, ready to take the afterbirth. They ate as fast as they could, ripping the carcass apart and tearing away mouthfuls of meat. The first vultures were overhead and a whooping call announced the first prowler – a hyena, but this was no ordinary animal. This was the head of the clan – the alpha female – Kikuto. She was here on the plains for the wildebeest calving, many kilometres south of her normal home range. It was worth the journey, though. While the food supplies up north were dwindling after the migration had left, down here in the south there was more than enough.

She looked the young lions up and down. They seemed unworthy even of her contempt. There was no love lost between lions and hyenas, and to her these two nonentities were worse than scum. They had no proper manes and they were killing small fry. She whooped again and several more hyenas appeared. They lunged forward at Mbili and Tatu in ones and twos, careful to keep clear of the lions' claws and jaws. More whoops brought many more of the clan, so that there were more than 20 hyenas surrounding the brothers. They, in turn, growled at the intruders and showed their teeth, but it was no good. There were far more than the two lions could hope to keep at bay. They made a hasty retreat. At that moment the hyenas surged forward and tore apart what remained of the calf. One ran off with part of a leg, another had the skull. In less than a minute, it was all gone.

Mbili and Tatu loitered nearby and watched the clan depart. After a brief chorus of whoops and cackles, they all ran off. Tatu went to look if any wildebeest meat remained. He sniffed around, but all that was left was blood on the ground. He looked up, and there was Kikuto looking down from the rise. She seemed almost to be sniggering, that is, if hyenas can snigger. But the image of his sister Moja being caught and devoured by a hyena flashed through his mind. He would have his revenge . . . some time. The hyena turned and, as he looked up again, she was gone.

For a few weeks, the brothers ate well. The wildebeest births had saved them from an uncertain future, and they were more efficient at bringing down their prey. They were becoming a force to be reckoned with, but they still had to mind their step. They were always on the territory of one pride or another and if they wanted to remain alive and well, they had to avoid any contact, let alone confrontation.

By mid-March, the wildebeest-birthing season was almost over. About 80 per cent of the population had given birth in just three weeks, with almost all the cows over three years old producing a calf. Most survived this, the first of life's traumas. Any born out of season were sure to be killed. They would not survive for more than a day. Without the glut of births and sated predators, they were easy targets. Again, the brothers were able to take their share, yet keep out of harm's way.

In April, the long rains arrived, the wildebeest calves were growing fast and there was change in the air. The herds were beginning to trickle northwards and westwards. When the trickle turned to a flood, Mbili and Tatu followed. They saw great lines of wildebeest stretched from one horizon to the other, accompanied by family parties of zebra and small herds of gazelles. As the brothers trekked with them, the landscape around them also changed. Massive rocky outcrops and piles of huge boulders were dotted across the plains – kopjes. They made good hiding places, and the brothers used them to rest by day, while they travelled at night.

Early one morning, when they were approaching their next refuge, Tatu was walking some way ahead of Mbili and, as he came up over a rise, little did he know that just ahead of him were a cheetah mother and her three tiny cubs. He would pose a real threat to her offspring so the mother was immediately on red alert. Tatu stopped, took a few paces forward, and stopped again. He looked out over the plains. There were lines of zebra and wildebeest on the horizon, and several giraffes were grazing beside a thorn tree. A family of warthogs ran for the safety of a ditch, while a small herd of gazelles grazed on a patch of green grass. He stood there for some time, seemingly without a care in the world.

The cheetah mother, meanwhile, was watching any move he made. She was sprawled out as flat as she could against the ground just 100 metres away. Her cubs were hiding behind some rocks nearby. Tatu had still not seen them. He started off once again, but he was walking in a direct line to where the cheetah mother was crouching. Surely, he would see her soon.

The cheetah looked around quickly, reassuring herself that her cubs were at a safe distance. They huddled together and were staying quite still and making no noise. Tatu came closer but he still had not spotted the mother. A group of gazelles ran behind him, a momentary distraction, but he did not react, merely plodded on. Then, almost on top of the mother, he spotted the movement of one of the cubs. It had tried to move behind a small bush and had given itself away. He turned towards the cub, staring intently at the spot, and started to stalk. The cubs were terrified.

Tatu was getting very close, but he still had not seen the mother. As he came alongside her, she stood up and adopted her threat position, her head low, her shoulders high. He saw her out of the corner of his eye and stopped, but he still stared directly at the cub. She turned her head quickly to check it had stayed where it was and advanced on the lion – it was like David and Goliath. The slender cheetah was dwarfed by Tatu, his adult mane making him look even bigger than he really was; but she was undeterred. She had to do something. Tatu walked steadily towards the cub, while its mother came to intercept him. She walked straight in front of him and Tatu was indeed distracted. He chased the mother instead of the cub. The cubs ran, but again he spotted the movement.

The mother saw where he was looking and tried to distract him again. Tatu, however, seemed to have lost interest. The cheetah went to her cubs and lay on the ground, her eyes fixed on the lion. He blinked, turned and walked away. Just then, Mbili came up and the two lions strolled together to the next pile of rocks. The cheetah and her cubs had had a narrow escape.

The brothers walked on, finding themselves at the entrance

of a gorge. They entered nervously, the rocky walls towering above them and a strange smell pervading the air. It was a fine morning and, as the sun began to climb higher into the sky, they saw small creatures – rock hyrax – clustered together on the upper ledges, basking in its warmth. It was they who had caused the stink, the result of generations of hyraxes depositing their droppings on the floor of caves and crevices. Around them, swallows were busily flying to and from mud nests built against sheer walls below rocky overhangs, and long-tailed starlings were chattering noisily in an African greenheart tree. Scurrying across bare boulders were agama lizards, and clouding the air were tsetse flies. It was different here, even just a few metres away from the grassland outside.

A family of baboons was firmly ensconced in a Euphorbia tree, tearing off the bark to get at the juicy pulp beneath. When they saw the lions, they barked their alarms and cleared out, clambering up the cliffs to outcrops higher in the gorge. The warning calls alerted a female leopard. The previous night she had caught and killed a wildebeest. Not only had she caught and killed it alone, but she had also stashed its carcass high in the branches of the tree. It was extraordinary how she was able to haul such a beast up the trunk, but she did and with no help from anyone else. Usually, the food would be safe there from most scavengers, but there were vultures circling around and a couple of eagles were moving through the branches, edging themselves closer to the kill. The leopard, though, had chased them away and she had settled down on a large branch next to the carcass, her legs and tail dangling in space. However, the eagles were persistent, and snatched pieces of meat, which they were taking to eat at leisure in neighbouring trees. At this, the leopard had had enough, lifted the carcass and began to move it to a place that was less accessible. But just as the wildebeest slipped from her grasp and fell to the ground, several zebras and gazelles rushed out of the surrounding undergrowth in blind panic. They had been spooked by something and, sure enough, out came Mbili and Tatu.

The leopard was safe enough in the tree, but this was her gorge and the lions were intruding. She made a screeching sound, and she snarled and hissed at them. They looked up and were ready to attack the spotted cat. Lions will kill leopards if they catch them. They are competitors. But more interesting was the smell of meat. Mbili quickly found the leopard's kill beneath the tree. Ignoring the protestations from above, they started to eat. For leopards, it is as difficult to keep their food as it is making the kill, and this leopard had no choice. She had to remain in the tree until the lions had finished, and that was likely to be a long while.

The long rains continued through May. Each day, in late afternoon, the heavens opened. It meant the grass was green and feeding for all the animals on the great migration was good. By now they had entered a new landscape – grassland with open woodland. It marked another phase in the wildebeest's lifecycle and another opportunity for the two nomads to capture an easy meal. It was the rut.

Wildebeest bulls are ready to mate at any time, but most get down to reproduction at full moon towards the end of the rains when all the animals are in tip-top condition, and Mbili and Tatu were, as usual, in the thick of it. They were now far from home and still had to keep an eye open for local prides. Each evening and at dawn, the pride males roared their proclamation of ownership, indicating to the two brothers precisely where they were located and, as long as they were not tempted to roar back, they were able to move in and out of a territory without the pride ever knowing they had been there. For now, though, their focus was less on calves and more on the bulls.

The bulls were chasing about constantly, herding females, mounting them or seeing off rivals. A male would approach either sex and, while calling, exhibit a rocking canter. Their call rate was far greater than during the rest of the year, and some were so worked up they frothed at the mouth. Bachelors even joined the territorial males and called with them, producing a chorus reminiscent of a bunch of frogs. Each of these territorial males rounded up a small herd of about 16 females and, for as long as they were present, the bull neither ate nor drank. Successful mountings were accompanied by a long, single belch, but if a female failed to stand still, the bull reared up on its hind legs in front of her, with his forelegs pointing at her. If she was not intimidated by this extraordinary courtship posture, she gave in. It was all a very exhausting business, during which bulls were less vigilant.

There was very little cover on the rutting ground, but the brothers kept out of sight as best as they could. They searched the herds for any bulls that were flagging, and after about an hour they located a possible target. He had been fighting full on with a rival. After bouts of tail swishing and horn sweeping, the two came to blows. Many times they smashed heads and dropped to their knees, thrusting forwards in an attempt to unbalance the opponent. But the challenger won, usurping the territory holder. The loser slumped to the ground. Mbili spotted the move, and began to stalk. Tatu followed his lead.

With their manes growing and thickening by the day, they were finding it increasingly difficult to remain unseen. It was one of the drawbacks of being a male lion and, as long as they were nomads, it would continue to be a problem. Once they had a pride of their own, they could leave the hunting to the females. They were better shaped for hunting. Males, with their impressive manes, were built for protecting their pride, especially their offspring. For now, however, their manes were nothing more than a nuisance, and Mbili's blond mane was especially a handicap as it was clearly visible from some distance away.

Nevertheless, the brothers were becoming successful hunters in their own right, and now they were about to take on an animal that was particularly strong, albeit more than a little tired. They crept closer, using any bit of cover they could find. The wildebeest had not seen them coming. It was facing away. Also, it had not noticed that all the other wildebeest were staring intently at the two lions. It should have been a giveaway. The bull turned its head. The brothers froze, and made to look like rocks. It worked. It turned back again. Mbili began his run. Tatu went off to one side. But some sixth sense told the wildebeest that something was wrong. It got to its feet, turned and seeing the two lions, tried to escape. It was too late. Mbili leaped on to its back and anchored his claws into its flanks. A moment later, Tatu slammed into its side. The wildebeest toppled with their weight. Mbili grabbed its throat, but Tatu was already tearing into the soft underside. It tried to struggle to its feet, but it was all to no avail. Within minutes it was suffocated. The brothers fed quickly, before other lions turned up. There was nowhere close by to hide the carcass so they had to eat as much as they could, as quickly as they could.

Without interruption, the two young lions were able to gorge themselves until sated. While they were eating a large number of pied crows and yellow-billed kites had gathered. They waited patiently on the periphery for the lions to finish. Mbili stopped feeding and sauntered for about ten metres and then flopped down on the ground. Tatu seemed reluctant to leave the remains of the carcass and lay right next to it. A line of crows advanced towards him, but every time he looked around, they retreated. The kites were more aggressive. They took to dive-bombing Tatu, and he was not best pleased. He got up and tried to cuff them, even jumping up to try and catch one. The commotion, however, attracted others.

Three large male lions had spotted them. This was their patch, and the brothers were trespassing. They moved smoothly and silently across the rutting ground. The herds of wildebeest parted and withdrew to let them through. There was no panic. They were not a threat to the wildebeest; they were on border patrol and about to evict the intruders.

About half-a-kilometre from the brothers the pride males halted and roared. Mbili and Tatu were up on their feet in an instant and this time they roared back. This was their first mistake. The three residents advanced. Mbili and Tatu stood their ground – their second mistake. The three lions were almost upon them when Tatu lost his nerve and ran. The lead lion, a powerful male with a full, dark brown to black mane, caught Mbili and cuffed him. The two rose up on their back legs, the older lion tearing and snarling at his adversary. Mbili disentangled himself and he ran too, the three males close at his heels. His full stomach was a distinct handicap, but he managed to keep ahead. His face was bleeding, the blood running down into his eyes, and he had deep and bloody scratch marks where the resident's claws had raked across his rump. He kept on running.

After about a kilometre, the residents dropped back. Mbili and Tatu continued as fast as their full stomachs would allow them, not full speed, but enough to take them clear of the pride males, and they did not look back. It had been a narrow escape, but their youth and speed had saved them. They dropped to a trot and then started to walk, making for a waterhole. Antelope and gazelles moved out of their way, but not far. The brothers' barrel-shaped tummies showed they had fed well and they would not be hunting again for a while. Nevertheless, the other animals kept a close eye on them. A lion they could see was less dangerous to them that a lion they could not.

Mbili went to the water's edge first. Tatu looked around. He did not want any more hidden surprises. Mbili crouched down, with his elbows out. His fat belly was flat on the ground as his pink tongue lapped up the cool water. He paused. Looked up. Tatu began to drink. They alternated – one down, the other watching. Mbili finished, got up, and licked the last drip from his chin. He headed for some acacia woodland, Tatu close behind, and there they lay down for the rest of the day and most of the night.

By June, the vanguard in the migration had reached the south side of a large river that bisected the plains. The nomadic brothers continued to follow these herds for it was their best source of food. By the time they had reached the river, however, most of the migration had already crossed. They were amongst the tail-enders, and they were milling about on the south bank, looking for a suitable crossing place. The river was not continuous but had deep pools and narrow channels, but it was still a barrier.

Mbili and Tatu strolled down to the water's edge to drink. They looked around to check for danger and then crouched, lowered their heads and began to drink. Mbili noticed a long, grey log floating in the river. He drank some more, looked up, and mysteriously the log had gone. He continued to drink. Tiny bubbles appeared on the surface. He paid no heed. Then, his world nearly came to an abrupt end. Without warning, the largest jaws he had ever seen came rushing out of the river and snapped shut just centimetres from his head. His lightning reaction just saved him from being dinner to one of the largest Nile crocodiles living on Earth, the undisputed champion of the river.

The primeval beast was all of six metres long and weighed 225 kilos. During his 40 or so years in the river, he had clawed his way to the top, and now he was here, in a fountain of spray, directly in front of Mbili. It was rare that he missed his target. His staring green eyes blinked and silently he slid back down into the river and was gone. Mbili sat dumbfounded. He was lucky to be alive. He and Tatu stared into the murky water. What else was down there? And, more importantly, how were they going to cross the river? Their mobile food service had already moved on. Somehow they had to get across and catch up with the migration. They walked up and down the river-bank, searching for a suitable place.

It was then that they came across more crocodiles, not in the water but on the bank. They were basking in the sun, their mouths partly open in order to lose some of the heat that they had absorbed. Even crocodiles are in danger overheating. They were also a distinct hazard for inexperienced lions, for the brothers had not seen crocodiles before. So, when they found a smaller one under a bush, it became something to investigate – was it edible?

Tatu, as usual, was fearless. He batted the crocodile on the nose, barely leaping back in time as its tooth-filled jaws swung round towards him. The two brothers backed away, stopping at a real log to sniff the breeze. The smell of crocodile was unfamiliar. They moved tentatively towards another of the beasts.

This time they circumnavigated the head end and stopped alongside its tail. Tatu seemed entranced by the strange creature, and simply stood and stared, ready in an instant to jump back should it move. Curiosity, though, got the better of him, and his inexperience was beginning to show again. He bent down to sniff at the long, armoured body. It did not move at first, then suddenly it twisted around and slid on its stomach back into the river. Tatu had been lucky the animal had not bitten him. They kept clear of the other crocs and flopped down under a tree beside the water, and there they remained during the heat of the day.

Come evening the river came alive. A heron glided in, flapped and settled on the far bank. A flock of sandgrouse, which had been disturbed by the passing herds from their early morning drink, set down at dusk instead. They crowded along the water's edge, oblivious to the dangers that could be lurking below. A kingfisher, balanced on a branch overlooking the shallows, was ready to plunge in pursuit of a small fish, and a party of Egyptian geese honked noisily before taking off for their evening roost. Frogs joined the evening chorus and croaked from the reeds, while one of the giant crocodiles, basking on a sandbank nearby, opened its mouth, its only movement for several hours. An Egyptian plover busied about its tooth-filled maw, plucking pieces of dead meat and parasites from between its teeth.

Mbili rose. Tatu likewise. With dusk approaching and the local pride most likely on the prowl, they had better go hunting now rather than in the night, and it was not long before they chanced upon an easy meal. All that could be seen above the long, brown grass was a pair of long, curved horns, the headgear of a male Grant's gazelle. The animal itself was lying in the grass, unaware of the approaching lions. Mbili and Tatu walked together at first, shoulder to shoulder, as if looking for mutual reassurance. Mbili then led the way, and they were able to stalk to within a few metres of their quarry. With just a few paces to go, the gazelle heard a footfall and rapidly got to its feet . . . but it was not quick enough. Mbili slammed into its side and knocked it over, while Tatu, carefully avoiding the sharp tips to the horns, grabbed it by the throat. The gazelle, though, was not finished. It rose to its feet, shaking Tatu off, leaving Mbili riding across its rump, its legs and hooves kicking out violently. The sheer weight of the lion, however, brought it down again. Its back legs buckled and Tatu re-applied the suffocating bite. The gazelle was soon dead; they fed well again that night. With full stomachs, they rested for the rest of the night and much of the following day, returning to the river in the evening to find a crossing place. Instead, they found a dead wildebeest.

The two nomads were not especially hungry, but nosed the carcass anyway. They sniffed at it and then lay down alongside it. They could eat it later. But, while they sat, crocodiles began to emerge from the water. They had spotted the food too and were intent on taking it. Mbili stood and walked around them, careful to keep out of the way of their jaws. He bit one of the crocs on the tail and jumped back as it arched its back and opened its mouth in defence. He returned to Tatu. The crocodiles, meanwhile, lined up on the beach, so that the two lions were on one side of the wildebeest and crocodiles on the other. The brothers flicked their tails nervously, just as one large crocodile walked straight up to the carcass and tried to take a bite. The lions leaped up and pawed him, but he lashed at them with his tail, sending Tatu flying across the sand. Several other crocodiles moved forward and latched on to the body, hanging on tight. The lions pulled from the other side, but there were too many of them. The brothers let go and the crocs had a tug-of-war between themselves, pulling the carcass asunder and swallowing large chunks whole. All the lions could do was watch.

With their food stolen from right under their noses, the brothers set out to find a crossing place that was safe from crocodiles. They did not have to look far. A series of large flat slabs provided stepping-stones across a narrow channel, and they were across . . . and they did not even get their feet wet.

For a while, the brothers lost touch with the migration. They had to take advantage of opportunities as they arose and they were not against stealing, especially from hyenas. One evening, they were camped out in a thicket, watching life going by, when they saw a gang of three hyenas grab a zebra foal. It had not long been born, but the mother was unable to help. The foal was pinned to the ground, but the hyenas hesitated momentarily and it jumped up and tried to escape. They pinned it down again, killed it and began to feed. At this, Tatu approached the three gluttons, slowly at first to assess their strength. He paused, and then ran headlong into the group, grabbing one by the shoulder and grappling with it to the ground. The others fled. He fell on his side, still holding on to the unfortunate beast, but the other two returned and succeeded in driving Tatu away. He ran to about 50 metres away, turned and waited. The injured hyena tried to raise its head but it could only roll over and over on the ground. Its companion sniffed at it, encouraging it to stand, but it could not. Its back was broken.

Mbili rushed the two survivors, singling out one for special attention. He ran alongside, preventing the hyena from turning, while Tatu came up from behind, extended his forepaw and tripped it up. As it fell it ensured its lethal jaws were pointing at the lions, enabling it to get to its feet and flee. The other hyena stood and watched, but Tatu turned back and began to chase it too. It hooked the hyena's rear foot, bringing it down. He grabbed its head and crushed its skull. Lifting the inert body, he carried some distance away and discarded it, before returning to Mbili, who had already started to tuck into the zebra foal.

The herds, meanwhile, had been following the rains northwards and, by September, when the brothers eventually caught up, they were prevented from going any further by an even bigger watercourse, and the water level here was certainly not low. Rains in nearby hills fed the swollen river so that in places it was a raging torrent. There was nothing for it – all the animals had to swim. It was a good place for an ambush.

Mbili and Tatu hid beside a likely crossing point. Along this stretch of the river, the water was contained between high, almost vertical-sided embankments, but a hippo track led down to the water, and nearby hundreds of wildebeest, zebra and gazelles were gathering, ready to cross. They would try to intercept their prey as it went down to the water. They watched and waited. One thing they had both learned during the past few months was patience. But the first animal they saw at the water's edge was not an obvious target for lions. A large lizard was working its way along the riverbank. It kept looking up, cocking its head to look at something high on the crumbling cliff face. This was no ordinary lizard. It was a monitor – a Nile monitor – and monitors have brains as well as brawn. This one was showing it.

All along the sheer bank there were holes, the entrances of bee-eater nest burrows, but the heavy rains and the river had undercut the cliff, causing the face to fall away. As the burrows were exposed, their contents dropped into the river or were piled up at the base of the cliff. All the monitor need do was look for places where the cliff had collapsed and then root around for the eggs and nestlings. It was having a successful day, but then

Tatu interrupted it. He sniffed at the monitor and was about to cuff it when the monitor turned and whipped its long tail across his face. Tatu jumped back with an audible 'whoof'. His eyes were stinging and his nose hurt. He went back to where Mbili was hiding. They would try for more familiar prey.

Tatu's little foray, of course, spooked the herds and so the brothers had to wait even longer for things to settle down. They hid in the undergrowth at the riverside, and were downwind of the crossing place so were unlikely to be detected.

At first, nothing came, but after a while, a small herd of Thomson's gazelles gathered at the top of the hippo track. They were understandably uneasy, but eventually the first animal made its way down to the water. It stopped and looked. The river must have seemed an insurmountable barrier, but even with their pencil-thin legs, gazelles can swim. Others joined it, and they edged closer to the water. All it needed was one to take the plunge and the rest would follow. Mbili and Tatu watched as the gazelles hesitated, but the two lions would have had to run too far across open ground before they reached the herd. The fleet-footed gazelles would have been away before they had a chance to grab one. They continued to watch instead.

One animal came right up to the river and leaped in. One by one, the others followed. The current was quite strong and so these relatively weak swimmers were carried downstream, but that was not the worst of it. The main hazard here suddenly made itself known. A large crocodile grabbed the leading gazelle by the head and dragged it under. More crocodiles appeared. The place was crawling with them. It was a massacre. Gazelles were plucked, drowned and dismembered. The reptiles queued up at each lifeless carcass, taking turns to grab a piece of meat and twist it off the body by spinning in a death roll. With the food held firmly in its mouth, they then pushed their head vertically out of the water and let gravity assist it down their throat.

But the gazelles kept jumping in. They seemed oblivious to the carnage in mid-stream. One after the other they leapt and they swam for all they were worth. Many of those that escaped the crocodiles were washed downstream, where steep banks prevented them from getting out. They collapsed from exhaustion and drowned too. Others made it. They clambered out on the other side and scrambled up the muddy hippo track. That's when Mbili and Tatu were suddenly on the alert. As the gazelles struggled up to the top of the bank, several lionesses that had been hiding there leaped out and grabbed them. They were from the local pride, a formidable group – the Tingatinga Pride, a pride they would come to know only too well, but for now they were a serious threat to the brothers' health. The river and nearby marsh was in their territory. They were on the other side of the river, but this did not bode well for the brothers. Mbili and Tatu remained hidden.

Later that day, the zebras arrived – several family groups. They too wavered at the edge. They were smarter than the gazelles. The stallions had spotted the crocodiles, and were searching the riverside for a safer crossing place. They began to congregate near a small cataract in the river, where white water cascaded over a line of submerged rocks. The crocodiles were unlikely to approach too close. The first stallion waded in. The water was soon up to his belly, and the current was tugging his legs, but he kept on his feet and was able to wade out on the other side. He whinnied, calling the rest of his family to follow. They entered the water. The larger animals found the going difficult, but they did not stumble. The smaller ones, though, were in real trouble. The fast-flowing water just picked them up and carried them over the rapids and downstream into the mouths of the crocodiles. Several went the same way, but most of the small herd made it across. They were leading a charmed life, for even the lions failed to appear. They were too busy finishing off their feast of gazelle.

And that was it for several hours. Everything was quiet. Crocodiles hauled out on to beaches. Urgent parents attended any bee-eater nests that had so far survived the collapsing riverbank. A handful or vultures and marabou storks picked at the remains of crocodile victims that had been washed ashore. All that could be heard was the sound of the river and the calls of birds in the riverside forest. Then a couple more zebras turned up. They were not with families, but two bachelors. They headed down to the river and, like the others, they paused at the water. Mbili saw the opportunity, and began to stalk. Tatu remained hidden, but was ready to rush them.

A vulture flapped. The zebras jumped back and dashed back up the track, one lagging behind the other. Mbili pounced. He placed both forepaws on the zebra's rump, his claws anchored into the flesh. His feet trailed on the ground. The zebra buckled with Mbili's weight and they both fell. Mbili was up first and had his weight firmly over his victim's head and neck. He shifted his position so that Tatu could bite at the throat. He hung on until the zebra was dead.

But they were in the open. They had to get the carcass under cover before the pride on the opposite bank saw them. Mbili grabbed the neck and straddled the body, dragging it into a stand of croton bushes. There they could get their breath before dismantling the body. Mbili was panting with all the effort, but Tatu was already licking the corpse. They had a fabulous prize and had snatched it from right under the noses of the local pride. They had done well. They were becoming very accomplished lions, indeed.

But that was not the end of the crossing. Not long after the young lions had eaten their fill, there was a strange but distant sound. It was clearly audible, a low-pitched hum. On the river, any crocodiles basking onshore slipped quietly into the water. They had picked up the vibrations through the ground, and knew exactly what was about to happen. Vultures and marabou storks dropped out of the sky and lined the trees along the riverbank. The lion pride looked up, and scattered to hide in bushes on the opposite bank. It was as if the audience was gathering to watch some extraordinary event, which is precisely what they were doing. Mbili and Tatu remained in their croton bush.

As the sounds came closer, the hum turned into an unruly chorus of snorting and grunting. The wildebeest had arrived – thousands of them. Their marching columns stretched back as far as the eye could see, their footfalls vibrating through the very earth itself. They were following the rains not only back and forth across the plains, but also on both sides of the river, and it was time for them all to cross to the other side. Now this drama was about to unfold and its audience was ready.

The first wildebeest stopped at the top of the riverbank and looked down into the water. A few ambled down the hippo track to the water's edge and began to drink. They were safe. The crocodiles would not attack them while they were on the shore. They knew better than that. They did not want to spook the frontrunners, or the wildebeest might cross elsewhere. There was more to the crocodile mind than they were given credit for. They either floated on the surface and did not move, or submerged and hung in the water, just their nostrils and eyes visible on the surface.

Increasingly, more wildebeest arrived. They packed the embankment above the river, and there were so many arriving that the ones behind began to push the ones in front. Some walked down the hippo track, while others were brought to an abrupt halt by the edge of the river cutting, a drop of several metres. The pressure continued to build up behind the front ranks until something had to give.

Whether it was pushed or whether it jumped, the first animal was in the water and the floodgates opened. Wildebeest began to pour into the river. The crocodiles let the first animals through. They were waiting for the mayhem that would shortly follow. The current carried the wildebeest downstream so, like the gazelles before them, they made landfall under a steep cliff with no exit points. This meant they also had to double back to reach the hippo track on the far bank. It was already chaos, and the main part of the herd had yet to cross.

On the near side, wildebeest surrounded Mbili and Tatu. The noise was deafening. But they were well hidden and all of the animals ignored them. Those on the high embankment, however, were faced with another hazard. The sheer weight of numbers was causing those on the edge of the cliff to be pushed off. They tried to scramble down, but the slope was too steep and they fell. Some broke legs as they landed and, failing to get up, they were trampled to death by the horde piling into the river.

A fallen tree obstructed animals trying to cross further up-stream. Some leaped on to it, slipped and were drowned where they fell. Others jumped over it and into the current, only to be washed downstream to the waiting crocodiles. They, in turn, grabbed anything that floated their way. One minute a wilde-beest was swimming, the next it disappeared below the surface. A crocodile performing its death roll was the only sign that anything had been there at all. Sometimes, a wildebeest appear-ing to swim against the current and the tide of animals was the unwitting victim of a crocodile attack. It was being dragged upstream. There was no escape.

Exhausted animals were hauling themselves out on the far bank, but the rocks were slippery and many slid back into the water only to be washed away. Others lost their footing and broke limbs and were left to die were they lay. A calf with a broken horn had become separated from its mother and had no idea which way to go. It walked about aimlessly at first, and then went back into the river where, in its confusion, it swam in the opposite direction to the rest of the herd. A large crocodile reared up, grabbed it by the rump and pulled it below.

More vultures arrived. They kept out of the way of the herd and gathered along the shore. Marabou storks stood alongside them, waiting for the pandemonium to subside before wading in to pick at the corpses. Bodies that had not been swept away were beginning to pile up in pools at the side of the river. There would soon be food for all the scavengers. For them the river crossing was an eagerly awaited bonanza. Vultures had flown several hundred kilometres from their nesting sites on the cliffs of distant mountains just to be here. With so much food, it was the best time for them to rear chicks.

Wave after wave of wildebeest continued to sweep down and into the river. The water was black with their struggling bodies. Nevertheless, each of the crocodiles could only take one wilde-beest at a time. The great majority survived the river crossing, some leaping over their stricken herd mates in the panic to reach the other side.

On the far bank, they streamed up the hippo track, but waiting for them was the Tingatinga Pride. They killed almost for the sake of killing, like a fox in a chicken coop. Their sensory systems were on overload. There were just so many animals and they were so easy to catch. On their side of the river, Mbili and

Tatu dared not move. If they caused a stampede now, with so many animals around them, they could be seriously injured or even killed themselves. They simply had to stay put.

After what seemed like an age, the back markers in the herd were across. The sounds of their snorting and grunting disappeared into the distance. Apart from the sound of running water and the bleating of the walking wounded, there was comparative silence. It was time for the scavengers. The vultures perched on bloated corpses, ripping through hides and extracting the meat, and the marabou storks picked, almost daintily, at open wounds with their huge bills. Jackals hurried between the bodies washed up on the shore, and kites and crows swooped down to take their share. They were all so intent on feeding that nothing made a sound. There was so much for all; even the vultures had stopped their squabbling.

With the sun high in the sky, the river area began to stink. In the heat, the bodies were already starting to decompose and putrefaction was setting in. Clouds of flies filled the air. The scavengers seemed not to notice. The monitor lizard returned and joined their numbers, flicking out its forked tongue, revelling in the smell and taste of death. Over 500 animals had died that day.

Mbili and Tatu ventured out of their refuge and saw the carnage. Having eaten their fill not so very long ago, they had no need to be part of the macabre scene. They began to slink away before they were spotted by the pride on the other side. However, as they reached the top of the embankment, Kikuto and her clan of hyenas appeared. This area was her home ground too. She glared at the two brothers, before leading her group to the river. Mbili and Tatu stared back. It was a standoff. Now was not the time for a fight, not with the pride so close.

The brothers turned and disappeared into the bush. There would be another day.

By November, after many river crossing, and huge loss of life, the rains drew all the survivors first to the south-east and then back to the south of the region, where they completed the migratory circuit on the short grass plains. The brothers followed the migration for every inch of the way. It was a sure source of regular food and so they continued to follow in its wake. And this became their life for the next couple of years. They avoided conflict with local prides, were always careful to hunt when others were resting, and scavenged from other predators when the opportunity arose. They were inveterate nomads, but there was change in the air. They were becoming stronger and they were gaining invaluable experience that would set them up for the next stage in their life. They were growing in confidence daily.

Their appearance was changing too. They each had a full mane, and they walked with a noble swagger. They were big boys now. They were almost ready to challenge resident males for the right to a pride, and one day during the dry season, when the migration was in the north of its range, they had an encounter that would take them one step nearer that goal.

CHAPTER FIVE

– The Challengers –

The brothers walked over the top of a rise, and there in front of them was an old lioness and a freshly killed wildebeest. She had just made the kill and was tucking into her feast when the two brothers barged in. They strutted over hoping to appropriate at least part of the carcass, but the old lioness had other ideas. She was not about to give up any of her food to a couple of upstarts. As they approached she bared her teeth and snarled aggressively, lunging at the two startled lions. They sat down, out of range of her fury while the old lady tore at the meat. Mbili was salivating at the thought of just a small piece, and Tatu was trying to work out how to sneak in and out again without getting hurt.

Things were not that simple, however. Over the rise came more lions – the local pride, but not the old lioness's, at least, not now. She was a nomad like the two brothers, so the moment she saw the other lionesses charging her, she fled. This was once her pride, but she had been ostracised, much like the brothers' mother. She hung around the edges of the territory, always keeping clear of the other lionesses and, through her own ingenuity and cunning, she was able to catch food for herself. In fact, she was a very successful hunter. Because she did not have to share, she often fed better than the pride females. She may have been a tough old lady, but she was not going argue with the entire pride. She was out of there.

Lucky for Mbili and Tatu, the local gang was intent on chasing her away and had failed to notice they were there at all. They ran straight past the place where they lay. They could only look on in astonishment as the drama unfolded, and they quickly crept away to a safe hiding place. Things were less comfortable for the old lioness. Some of the residents were hot on her heels, but she kept on running. She was surprisingly fast, but after more than a kilometre and rather breathless, she stopped to face her pursuers. Panting heavily, she glared at the residents bearing down on her. At first, she put her head down in submission, and placed her backside firmly against the ground so she could not be attacked from behind.

The resident females charged. Roars and snarls filled the air and six of them surrounded the old lioness, lunging and swiping with their forepaws. Two tried to bite and claw at her rear end, while two others slapped at her face. She leaped at one, raking her face with her claws, only to be bitten and clawed on the rump in return. She whirled round, trying to protect her rear and was bitten by the two on the other side. She was in serious trouble, and she knew it. She lay down for a moment's rest, then responded again, but each time she moved the rest of the crew piled in and she was bitten severely. Deep gashes appeared on her face and sides, and large chunks of her fur went flying through the air.

And so the attack went on. The rest of the pride had gone to assist their pride mates and taunt the intruder. It meant that Mbili and Tatu found themselves left alone with a dead wildebeest. What was a self-respecting lion to do? They quickly tore at the carcass, ripping away as much meat as quickly as they could. They had to out of there before the resident females returned, or they would be allotted the same vicious treatment, and the pride had the advantage of numbers.

The pride lionesses stopped fighting, but they still encircled the old lady. At the slightest move from either side, both snarled and showed their teeth. They were sizing up each other, when two of the residents stood and tried to position themselves behind the rival lioness. They were actually on either side of her, but each time they tried to manoeuvre into an attack position, she swung around. One of the pride lunged forward, she countered and then made a run for it. Again, she ran for her life, but the others were quickly after her. She doubled back and stopped, panting heavily. She was exhausted. Her pursuers came to a halt too. It was another standoff.

With the battle far from over, Mbili and Tatu were able to gorge themselves. The pride lionesses, meanwhile, had taken themselves into the shade, but the intruder was kept out in the open, under the glare of the late morning sun. Two of the lionesses sauntered over and she snarled at them. They lunged at her and she fled. She jumped a stream and ran rapidly up and over the opposite bank. The residents did not give up. Over the stream they went too, and they continued the chase. The intruder stopped, and again she turned to face her pursuers. She grimaced, baring her teeth, but was too tired to make any sound.

All were now in the open and it was getting on for midday, the hottest time of the day. The pursuers decamped to a fallen tree, which offered a little shade, but the old lioness was clearly uncomfortable. She was foaming at the mouth and saliva dripped from her chin. All were panting. A couple of the lionesses fell asleep, and when the old lady got up slowly and slunk away, the others just watched her go and did nothing. She had survived their ferocity, but she would be careful not to overstep the mark again. In fact, such were her wounds she could barely walk. Her tail was broken, and there were deep gashes at the top of her legs. She made it to the edge of an acacia thicket and dropped to the ground. She closed her eyes and slept a deep sleep, lucky to be alive.

When she awoke, she looked up and there were the two brothers looking down at her. Her heart jumped a beat. Was this the end? She had barely the energy to react. The boys just stared. In reality, by drawing away the resident pride females, this old lioness had saved them from a serious beating, and now she lay there injured and in considerable pain. Mbili walked up to her battered body and began to lick the blood from her open wounds, more for the salt than for any altruistic reason. Tatu stood guard, searching the horizon for signs of the pride lionesses.

The boys stood over the old lioness for several days – as long as it took for her to recover, but recover she did. This was Grandi, and her story was remarkably similar to that of their mother's. After she was ousted from her pride, she had lived on its fringes. She had acquired a companion, a magnificent lion with a pure black mane, but he had been a loner too. Without a male companion to back him up in fights, he had not stood a chance in the lion's world. A male alone with a lioness could not take over a pride. In the same way that the pride lions had killed their mother's escort, the black-maned male had been killed too, and she had been forced to survive on her own. Time and again she had tried to return to her pride, but time and again she had been rebuffed. It was a strange coincidence. Now, she was here with Mbili and Tatu, and it seemed to be right. Fate had played a hand in events that day.

Since the feast on the stolen wildebeest, all three had not eaten for several days. They had to feed up. It was late morning.

The air was heating up. Resident prides would be sleeping off whatever they had caught and eaten the previous night. It was a good time to hunt, and now they were three, their chances of bringing down prey successfully had just increased significantly. And not only that; they could tackle things a great deal bigger.

Their first foray together was right on the Tingatinga Pride's doorstep. The young male buffalo was no more than a wavy outline in a shimmering heat haze. It was alone. The rest of the herd was some distance away. It was dallying, its attention taken up by a particularly attractive stand of long, fresh grass. It was, however, a fearsome target. It may have been a young animal but its head was broad with a wide, wet muzzle, its ears large and drooping and fringed with long, brown hair. Across its forehead was a thick, bony shield ending in a pair of formidable up-curved horns. The boss was still in two halves, indicating a bull yet to reach maturity.

Grandi's head was held steady, her eyes fixed on the target. The only visible movement was her shoulder blades moving up and down. Mbili and Tatu both thought of their mother. The intensity of the old lioness's concentration reminded them very much of her.

Grandi led the attack, while Mbili and Tatu followed her every move. She caught up with the young bull and leaped on to its rump, her forelegs like grappling irons clamped on either side of its back. Her back legs pushed hard against the ground so she vaulted up and on to its back. Like a rodeo rider on a bucking bronco, she hung on before grabbing the buffalo's neck in her vice-like jaws and gradually transferred her weight to one side. She slid down its flanks, holding tight with her teeth, and with the claws of her forepaws anchored on its shoulders. The buffalo turned to the right, desperately trying to shake the big cat off, but she hung on. Round and round they went in a macabre waltz. With Grandi hanging to one side, the animal was in danger of toppling over, but it spread its legs and planted its feet firmly on the ground. It croaked loudly.

Mbili and Tatu stood off at first, but when Grandi slid around the buffalo's head, Tatu jumped on to its back, hoping his weight would push the beast over. He sunk his teeth into the back of its neck and, with his claws firmly imbedded in the buffalo's back, he hung on tight, but it stood defiantly, its bellowing becoming all the more frantic. Grandi bit hard into the animal's throat, trying to suffocate it. Mbili suddenly realised what he should do. He grabbed either side of the buffalo's head and put his mouth over its muzzle so it could not breathe. All three hung on until their victim slowly sank to its knees and then fell to one side.

By this time, the animal's distress calls had alerted the rest of the herd. They raised their heads, smelled the air and looked intently in the direction of their stricken herd mate. However, with Mbili covering the buffalo's mouth and nostrils, it could no longer call out. The other buffalo were hesitant, but gradually a consensus seemed to be reached and they began to walk towards Grandi and the two brothers. They, in the meantime, had started to feed, and they were reluctant to leave their prize, even in the face of a gang of aggressive bulls.

Some of the herd sniffed at the dead buffalo's back. The lions watched them from over the top of the corpse, while they were working at the softer underside. Tatu gave a perfunctory snarl and bared his teeth, but it had little effect. The buffalo snorted in return, but the three lions refused to move. Eventually, the herd turned and walked away, breaking into a trot after a few metres. Why they did not attack was a mystery, but it meant that the lions could get on with their food without another fight.

After feeding, it was time to drink, so the three companions went to a nearby stream. Other game, even those animals no more than a few metres away, ignored them. They would not be hunting for a good few hours, and the other animals knew it. But, when they returned to the remains of the carcass, a group of jackals were tucking in. Tatu was not going to let them steal his hard-fought meal. One charge and they scattered, but there was one that was particularly persistent.

The jackal waited for a chance to dart in. It fussed around the lions and was becoming a minor irritation, but it had not reckoned on Tatu's fiery temper. The young lion hissed and snarled at the jackal, baring his large canine teeth. It then made an unfortunate mistake – it started to run. Tatu's natural reaction on seeing an animal running away was to chase it. He took off at high speed, and chased after it, matching every jink the jackal made and finally tripping it up with his forepaw. Instead of delivering the coup de grace, he left the jackal unharmed and returned to the kill. The jackal picked itself up and barked defiantly at Tatu. The lion ignored it. It had had a lucky escape. However, the scavengers were beginning to over-whelm Grandi and the two brothers by sheer numbers, so they reluctantly gave way, at least, for the moment. Immediately, an unruly gang of vultures pounced on the carcass and an eagle swooped overhead, all hoping to pilfer some of the spoils. The jackals became bolder and tried to chase the vultures away, and then the first hyena turned up.

However, even though they were sated, Tatu was not going to give up the kill to hyenas. He recovered the remains and stood guard. The vultures were forced to stand around like a bunch of spectators with hunched shoulders. They flapped aggressively at each other, competing with their neighbours for the best place to be should the lion give up its prize. Jackals continued to run around excitedly, ready to rush in at the slightest hint of a snatched morsel. But then more hyenas arrived. They came in ones and twos, but soon 20 or 30 were gathered around. They kept their distance at first, cackling and whooping to bring up even more of their numbers. Last to appear was Kikuto. Her staring eyes, set in a head more reminiscent of gargoyle on a church roof, glared at Tatu. Her mouth was partly open, revealing rows of teeth that could slice through flesh, sinew and even bone. Her surprisingly small head was set on a thick neck atop a back that sloped down steeply to her rear quarters. Her bushy tail stood erect. She loped over towards Tatu. He rose, lunged forward half-heartedly and gave a perfunctory roar and a snarl. Then he left the carcass to the horde. The lions' bellies were full. It was not worth the effort, so the three companions simply walked away and left them. Mbili looked back to see Kikuto watching their departure. He turned and trotted to catch up with Tatu and Grandi. Fortunately, the Tingatinga Pride failed to appear.

It was not long afterwards – no more than a couple of days – that the three companions returned to the riverside. From the roars they heard each morning and evening, they detected that the prowess of the two resident males appeared to be waning. Mbili and Tatu began to roar back. They lowered their heads, arched their backs, drew in their flanks and, as the muscles of their throats swelled up and their chests widened, they pushed out their muzzles and, with eyes half closed, caused the most extraordinary sound to rip across the savannah. Their deep, guttural roars were followed by a series of grunts carried straight to the core of the Tingatinga Pride's territory. The resident males would have been in no doubt that Mbili and Tatu were there and they meant business. For the next few days, they traded roars at dawn and again at dusk, and on one cool but sunny morning the contest came to a head.

The pride males stood and roared. They scratched the ground with their hind feet and scent-marked nearby bushes, although their hearts seemed not to be in it. They were once proud and noble beasts, but now they felt old and tired and were just going through the motions. Several nomads had tried to take over their territory, and the fighting was beginning to show. Their manes had become scraggy, with large pieces missing, and their faces were scarred and their bodies thin and drawn. The pride was hunting well, but the old males were always last at the kill, and they received the worst of the deal.

Mbili and Tatu were about half a kilometre away. They looked magnificent, almost royal. Mbili's blond mane had a black border and Tatu's had become much darker altogether. The full mane not only protected them in fights but also made them seem much larger and imposing. It was also a sign to members of the opposite sex that they had strong genes and would make good fathers. Yet, even though they had almost reached maturity, the spots on their legs and flanks, which were so prominent when they were cubs, were still faintly visible. As they roared back, they began to move forward, turning sideways occasionally to show how big and impressive they were. They swaggered more than walked, each with his head erect and his eyes fixed on the opposition. Grandi was a little way behind them. She roared too, but was careful to stay out of the fight. This was something the brothers had to do all by themselves.

Mbili broke into a trot. Tatu followed. The resident males stood firm. The two sides exchanged roars just one more time, but neither side backed down. The brothers charged. In seconds, they clashed. The noise was deafening, but the fight brief. Mbili's opponent turned and fled. Tatu's continued to fight, but was soon on his back with his feet drawn up in submission to protect his vulnerable underside. Nevertheless, Tatu continued to lay into him, and soon deep cuts appeared on his body and across his face. Large chunks of his mane littered the floor. Realising he was defending alone, he freed himself from Tatu's onslaught and staggered away, following his companion. The brothers chased them for over a kilometre before standing and roaring at them. It was a proclamation of victory, and it warned the defeated males to never return. They scent-marked nearby bushes, and then came together and rubbed heads. The brothers had won the territory, now they had to win over the rest of the pride.

Grandi caught up with Mbili and Tatu, and together they went to the place where the rest of the pride was waiting for the outcome of the battle. The lionesses with young cubs rounded up their offspring and left. They would set up their own pride elsewhere. If they stayed, the incoming males would have killed all the cubs in order that they became sexually receptive and ready to mate as soon as possible. Mbili and Tatu were not going to look after another lion's offspring. The exodus, however, saved the inevitable bloodletting.

This meant that there were five adult females left in the pride, as well as some older offspring. The sub-adult males had already made themselves scarce. If they had stayed, Mbili and Tatu would probably have driven them away at best and killed them at worst. Four of the sub-adult females remained, while the rest left with their mothers and younger brothers and sisters. Those that stayed gathered together, ready to confront the new masters. The first meeting was not that friendly. As the two brothers approached, Grandi dropped back again. They walked straight up to the lionesses, but were greeted with snarls and hissing. One of the older females – known as Old One Eye on account of her once slamming into a zebra's hoof – lunged at them, her ears back and her teeth bared. The others moved up beside her. They were ready to defend their territory, but the brothers were far bigger and considerably stronger.

Mbili stood firm, Tatu right beside him. Two of the females inched forward. Mbili roared at point-blank range. It was so loud the sound must have gone straight through them. They jumped back, chastened but still hostile. Tatu scraped the ground with his hind claws and urinated on the ground. The two lionesses lunged at him and one was cuffed on the side of her face for her trouble. Two more came up alongside and Tatu backed down. Both the brothers moved a few metres away and sat, staring intently at the ground. It was time for Grandi to make her entrance.

She marched forward towards the most aggressive pride members, two of the lionesses who had taunted and attacked her not that long ago. She walked very deliberately and without any hesitation, as if she belonged, which in a way she did. These two were actually relatives of hers – cousins – and now she was re-establishing herself in the family. Against all the odds, the lionesses relented. Grandi rubbed heads with each of them in turn. She was back in a pride again. The two conquerors, however, had still to be accepted by this close band of sisters and cousins.

The impasse went on for several days, but it was important that the brothers won over the pride females. Sometimes it could take months, or even years, for a pride to settle down after a takeover, but with Grandi's help it seemed as if the brothers would not have long to wait. Nevertheless, their acceptance was gradual. The breakthrough came when both Mbili and Tatu were allowed to join the pride at rest, without being greeted by a barrage of snarls and hisses. First to relent was Old One Eye. Then there was Umbu and Msichana, two young sisters, and their cousins Chipipi and Chica. Grandi brought the count to six lionesses, making it a good medium-sized pride.

The pride itself had been seriously disrupted. The split would be permanent. The females and cubs who left during the takeover would never return. They were likely to create a new pride of all females and cubs and, at some point in the future, it could be in direct competition with the group that remained, especially if nomadic males joined them. For the moment, though, they would have to live in the no-man's land between pride territories and eke out a living as best as they could. How many of their cubs would survive in this in-between world is anyone's guess.

For Mbili and Tatu it was a major change in the way they lived too. Now that they had a pride and a territory, they had regular ambush and sleeping's sites, as well as safe havens in which any future cubs could hide. The boundaries of their territory, though, were not well defined. On the east side, the edge of the territory was clearly marked by a river and marsh, but to the north were hills and, to the south and west, the plains where the boundaries were, to all intents and purposes, invisible. And, other prides – some powerful and others not so threatening – surrounded them, each occupying its own patch of savannah or woodland. They ranged in size from the small and secretive Kilima Pride in the hills, with just a handful of lionesses and two relatively old lions, to the powerful Makali Pride on the other side of the river, which had three strong, young males and half-a-dozen mature females, together with a handful of juveniles and cubs.

The brothers had to scent mark the boundaries often and roar at least twice a day to indicate that the territory was occupied. During the night, they traded roars with the males of the other prides. The neighbours had detected a change in the fortunes of the Tingatinga Pride and were testing the waters. From now on it was the brothers' job to keep them out and to chase away any others who might threaten or endanger their pride; and while *they* protected the pride and its territory, the females were left to hunt and rear cubs. The brothers had, in effect, almost become parasites, relying largely on the lionesses for their food. They also spent most of their time together, rather than mixing with the rest of the pride. They would lie separately, enjoying each other's company . . . except, that is, when the females came on heat, and then the competition between the brothers began to hot up.

When the first female was receptive, Mbili and Tatu fought seriously for the first time in their lives. Mbili won that first bout, and Tatu the second. Within days of each other, the five females were ready to mate. If they failed to conceive, they would have been ready again in about 16 days, but all the lionesses became pregnant. It kept the boys busy, for they were tied up with each prospective mother for about four days each, and they had to patrol their boundaries and be ready to attack any intruders in between times. The neighbours were especially inquisitive about what had happened. It was an exhausting time, but being in a pride had its advantages.

Surprisingly, hunting together was not necessarily one of them. A successful pride might have been able to bring down animals that were bigger than an individual lion could manage alone, and a group of six lions was twice as successful in catching prey, but the meat had to be shared. A lioness hunting large prey with others obtained no more food than a lion hunting smaller prey alone, sometimes significantly less. The real advantage came with the rearing of cubs. As all the females came into heat at roughly the same time, all the cubs were also born within days of each other. They could be reared together and protected more easily from nomadic males and predators, such as hyenas, by the entire pride. Pride females also had a better chance of defending their hunting territory and defending their kills against scavengers. It meant that cubs brought up in a pride had a better chance of survival than any reared by a single mother. Even so, a quarter of all cubs failed to make it to their first birthday, usually due to malnutrition.

Unlike wolf packs or hyena clans, there was no hierarchy within the pride. Mbili and Tatu could not be said to be leaders. They were there to procreate and protect – that was all. And all the females were closely related – mothers, daughters, sisters, cousins and aunts and they all had equal status. There was no alpha male or female. In fact, these related lionesses were really 'the pride'. While pride males came and went the female line remained constant. It was always the female cubs that would comprise any future pride. Mbili and Tatu had just three to four years as the resident males at best; then they would be ousted like their predecessors. It was a very short time for them to sire cubs and continue their line.

And so it was that Mbili and Tatu's first cubs were born – about three-and-a-half months after mating. The pride moved to a part of their territory that was favoured for giving birth, within the marsh on the eastern boundary. It was a large swampy area, with dense stands of reeds and croton bushes interspersed with muddy pools. It was fed by a spring that drained water from the nearby hills. Initially, the mothers retired to their favourite spots within the marsh and did not bring the cubs to meet the rest of the pride until they were a couple of weeks old.

The onset of family life also meant another change. While the cubs were small the pride had to remain in one area. The lionesses could not travel far or the cubs would have been left behind. The brothers, though, had to patrol the territory. The three lions of the Makali Pride were especially adept at commandeering not only neighbouring lands but also the next-door females. They had already taken over the territory to their east, the males commuting between the two prides, and before the brothers had arrived they had had designs on the Tingatinga Pride territory to their west. For the moment, though, they left Mbili and Tatu alone, and remained on their side of the river.

With the very young cubs and their mothers tied to the marsh for a few weeks, finding food for themselves and the two brothers was mainly down to Grandi and Old One Eye, two of the most experienced and accomplished hunters on the plains. Neither was fertile so they would never have cubs. Grandi had had a particularly harrowing time when she was pregnant the first time, the stress of being attacked frequently by the females of the old Tingatinga Pride causing her to abort violently. Unfortunately her system was damaged and she was unable to conceive again. Old One Eye was getting just too old. She had been a good mother, but now she left that to the younger lionesses. They were both, nevertheless, tough and agile predators, having lost none of their hunting sparkle when out on the plains.

Mbili and Tatu had come into the Tingatinga Pride area when following the migration, and the herds were still there, criss-crossing the river that formed their pride's eastern boundary. Sometimes they were in one territory and other times in the neighbouring land; but now there were lines of wildebeest and zebras as far as the eye could see, and all streaming towards the river. There was to be another crossing. While the other lionesses were in confinement, Grandi went out either with Old One Eye or by herself. The boys were nowhere to be seen.

On this occasion she was out hunting alone when she stumbled on a huge group of wildebeest that had gathered on the riverbank. They were about to cross. Grandi positioned herself close to the most likely crossing point, making sure that she was concealed below the lip of the bank, but then she saw a male leopard. She drew back into a thicket on the river's edge and peered out.

The leopard walked casually through a gully and then waited below a bush, scanning the riverbank for signs that the herd was on the move. They were still grazing, so he eased himself up over the embankment and along behind some bushes. His spotted coat blended in so well with the dappled light that he was almost invisible. As he reached a good hiding place, one of the wildebeest began to walk down towards the water. It was about 20 metres away and alone. The leopard bunched himself up, ready to charge, but then changed his mind, went back up the riverbank and joined the stream of animals heading for another crossing place upstream. The first ambush site had been too open. He would have been seen before he had had a chance to reach the nearest wildebeast. The leopard followed the flow, always careful to remain hidden behind bushes and trees. Grandi followed at a discrete distance.

Zebra were first to arrive at the water's edge. They gathered in family parties on the rocks at the crossing, until one of the stallions deemed it safe to cross. He led the way, the rest of his family following close behind. There were no crocodiles here. It was too narrow and too shallow. Other families took their turn, crossing in an orderly fashion; very different from the chaos of the wildebeest crossing that was to follow.

While the new crossing place was perfect for the large herds, it was even less suitable for a predator to attack than the first site. The leopard crawled almost flat to the ground as close as he could get without revealing himself, but there were still many metres of open ground to cover if he should charge. Again, he bunched itself up as the zebra cleared the crossing and the first few wildebeest were working their way down the bank. Grandi, who was not that far away, eased herself forward but still did not reveal herself. The smaller cat was searching for a zebra foal or wildebeest calf, but that was going to be made all the more difficult as the wildebeest did their usual thing – they were spooked and started to stampede.

Wildebeest were running in all directions. Some crossed hurriedly, while others were reluctant to clamber down. The leopard ran along the riverbank. In the confusion, he could move in the open and still not be seen. He made straight for the narrowest point, where wildebeest were streaming through, but by the time he got there the last of that particular batch was disappearing up and over the other bank. He was late again. The herd had run out. Grandi relaxed but continued to watch.

The rest of the herd, meanwhile, had doubled back and were contemplating the original crossing point. A zebra stallion walked confidently down the hippo trail to the water's edge and began to drink. The leopard also ran back, almost bumping into Grandi on the way. Then he watched from the cover of some bushes. Wildebeest and zebra numbers were beginning to build once more. They had gathered at the top of the track, unsure as usual whether to cross or not, when a group of Thomson's gazelle walked down to join the zebra. The first one passed close to where the leopard was hiding but he was biding his time, waiting for just the right moment.

More gazelles filed passed, while the first in the line waded through the water and ran quickly up the opposite bank. The leopard went for the third, a large male. He burst from his hiding place and the gazelle took off, racing downstream along the side of the river. The leopard chased after it, but the unfortunate creature leaped straight into a rock wall and fell stunned into the water. The cat dived straight in after it, grabbing it by the throat and trying to haul it out of the water. He needed all his strength to get the body on to the bank, while the prey all the while was struggling to escape. He let go for a second, clambered on to the bank, and then turned and grabbed the gazelle by the muzzle. There the cat rested, his mouth clamped tightly around the gazelle's mouth and nostrils. It was suffocated in minutes so, after shaking the water out of his fur, the leopard was able to haul the body on to the riverbank with no risk of it running away. His task was not over yet, though.

The cliff with which the gazelle had collided was directly behind, so he had to haul the heavy body over jagged rocks before reaching cover. For every step forward there were two back, as the body snagged continually but, centimetre by centimetre, the leopard carried it higher, every muscle in his body working overtime. Finally he dragged the carcass into dense vegetation where it could not be seen by other predators or scavengers and, after a short rest, he began to pluck the fur in order to get at the meat below.

He fed for no more than a few minutes, abruptly left his food, and disappeared down a large warthog burrow. The reason was soon clear. Grandi had left her hiding place and had designs on the leopard kill. The leopard clearly felt unsafe where he was and made a bolt for the woodland. The lioness snarled loudly and gave chase. The leopard made for a rather spindly tree and almost flew up the trunk. He was just out of reach, but had to keep as still as possible lest he break the branches and fall to the ground and instant death at the hand of Grandi, who stood frustrated at the bottom. She walked around for a while, looking up into the branches, but she was not a climber. There was no way she could get the leopard now, so she sauntered back to the kill.

With the lioness preoccupied, the leopard quickly came down and spirited himself away. He made for the river and a favourite fig tree whose thick branches arched over the river. He would be safe there, and not a moment too soon. Mbili and Tatu appeared. It was time to eat, care of their newfound rival. The three of them tucked into the leopard kill before other scavengers arrived. Right on cue, however, the first vulture dropped down and sat in a nearby tree. Then another . . . and another, until there were 40 or 50 gathered around waiting for a chance to get at the carcass, and then there was the familiar whooping of a hyena. It was one of Kikuto's clan, but their leader was not among them. As usual, they taunted the lions, trying to distract them for just a second; all that was needed for one of them to rip off a leg or a mouthful of flesh. But Tatu was not having it. He suddenly ploughed into the group, grabbed one by the head and bit into its skull, piercing its brain. It died instantly and Tatu left it where it had fallen. He was not into dining on hyena flesh. The vultures could have that and leave the lions alone. No sooner had he turned than the horde pounced. The body was stripped clean in less than an hour. The other hyenas slunk away.

The next day, with a few mouthfuls still left on the gazelle carcass, the three lions ate what they could and then went back to the marsh. The first of the females with cubs had yet to appear. The babies were still too young to be moved very far, so they remained hidden amongst the reeds. Some of the new mothers were visiting each other, but Grandi, Old One Eye and the two brothers were excluded for the time being. By living apart from the pride during the first weeks of a cub's life, it learned the sounds and smells of its mother, which would become important when it was caught up in the everyday hustle and bustle of a busy pride that was always on the move. It was useful to know exactly who its mother was.

So Mbili and Tatu went about their duties. They strutted out of camp burdened by their newly-found self-importance. It was time for them to patrol the territory, scent mark the boundaries and generally ensure that the territory was not harbouring intruders or open to incursions from neighbouring prides. Mbili walked up to a prominent bush and rubbed his head through the foliage before turning and squirting a spray of fresh urine. These scent marks would last for many days, even weeks, semi-permanent markers that delineated their territory. Tatu followed suit, except that after the head rubbing part he settled down for a rest under a bush. And that was it for the day . . . lions are extraordinarily lazy.

Six weeks after they were born, the first cubs emerged from their nursery hideaway. Their mother introduced them to the other members of the pride, but she was noticeably wary. Grandi and Old One Eye were allowed to approach, but when Mbili or Tatu came too close to the cubs, she snarled and showed her teeth. One of them was their father, but their mother was taking no chances. The same was true when the other mothers and their newborn cubs appeared. There were 15 in all, shared between five females. They almost formed a pride within the pride. The mothers hung out together and they pooled resources. They even suckled each other's cubs. In fact, it was sometimes difficult to see which cub belonged to which mother. Cubs snuck in alongside their pride mates and took a top-up from an aunty as well as from their own mothers. But every time one of the brothers walked towards their offspring the lionesses would stand in his way, forcing him to stay clear. The mothers were very tetchy, and this went on for a couple more weeks.

Eventually, it was the cubs themselves who broke the deadlock. The pride males fascinated them. They rummaged about in their luscious manes, bit their tails and generally made a nuisance of themselves. Mbili usually took it in his stride, but Tatu had a tendency to be irritable. He showed his teeth at any youngster that dared play around him, and bit down – albeit softly – on the little one's head. It was all a part of learning, though. The cubs had to be taught the etiquette and language of the pride. Body language, as well as the different sounds that lions make, had to be learned, in order that pride members knew how to behave in the company of other lions. All of the adult members of the pride were lethal killing machines and so they had developed a sophisticated recognition system that kept order within the pride.

As the cubs gained confidence, their mothers relented increasingly and allowed them to play with Mbili and Tatu without concern for their safety, and the two brothers made the nursery area their own resting place between eating and border patrols. The pride also began to hunt together. The mothers joined the two older females, leaving the cubs in a crèche in the care of one of their number. It was Grandi, however, who often initiated the chase, and sometimes even the brothers joined in. It meant they could bring down animals that one or two of them alone would be unable to kill.

And so it was early one evening when most of the Tingatinga Pride emerged from the shade. They walked in a ragged group through the long grass, heading towards the wildebeest herd scattered across the plain ahead. They approached from behind a stand of low bushes and trees, so the wildebeest were quite unaware that they were coming.

Grandi led the advance. With her ears facing forwards and her head low, she eased herself around the bushes and out on to the plain. Her back was visible above the grass stems but she was still mainly concealed from view. She hesitated briefly and stared intently at the herd, searching for the weak or the infirm. She could see topi and zebra as well as wildebeest, so she was spoiled for choice. She watched as many of the herd as she could, stalking them when their heads were down and freezing when any one looked up. If she spooked just one, the rest would flee. She moved deliberately and very slowly.

A male topi stopped feeding. Something was wrong; he could sense it . . . but he could not see the lionesses, nor could he smell them. Grandi slowed to a stop, waited for the topi to lower its head. As it did so, she edged forwards in a smooth gliding motion, her eyes locked on to the vigilant buck. One false move and the hunt would be over. She froze once again. A young buffalo had moved close to where the pride was hidden. There was a danger that it would not only give the game away, but it might charge as well. All the lionesses remained motionless as it walked slowly past Grandi. She turned. The pride had found a new target.

Just as it came alongside Grandi, the buffalo raised its head. It could smell lion. It stood stock still, like a large dark statue. It sniffed, licked its nose and sniffed again. It looked without turning its head. It grunted once, and shook its head. It walked deliberately towards Grandi. It stretched its neck, sniffed again. It knew the old lioness was there and continued towards her. Their eyes met. Both stared. They were no more than a few metres apart.

Grandi lunged forward. The buffalo flinched and then charged. Grandi ran, almost sideways like a crab, turning her head back towards her assailant, goading it to chase her. The rest of the pride was still hidden in the long grass. The buffalo could see only one lioness, and it was intent on chasing her away. Just then, Old One Eye joined her. Confronted by two cats, the buffalo turned and ran. Grandi ran too. She caught up and leaped on to its back, riding it like a jockey on a racehorse for a few paces before jumping down to the ground.

By now, the other lionesses had joined the pursuit. So had Mbili. He jumped on to the buffalo's back and sunk his teeth into the back of its neck, his claws firmly anchored on each side of its neck. The animal bucked, but Mbili stayed put. Grandi straddled its rump, but let go immediately as hooves were flailing in all directions. Mbili leaped off too. The buffalo ran a few metres, but three of the lionesses jumped on it in turn. Each rode it for a few seconds, and then jumped off again.

The buffalo kept turning almost on the spot, first one way and then the other, its legs kicking out and its horns brandishing from side to side. The lionesses were careful to keep clear of the head end and concentrated their attacks on the rump with another wave of attacks. As Old One Eye jumped on the buffalo's back, Grandi managed to get under its head with her forelegs hanging on to its neck, her mouth firmly over the buffalo's muzzle. She was trying to suffocate the beast, if only she could hang on.

With Grandi firmly in place, the others piled on and slowly the buffalo toppled. It struggled to get up but the weight of lions kept it down. All around, the wildebeest had stopped feeding and were turned towards the drama unfolding in front of them. They watched in silence as it reached its horrific climax. Mbili and the lionesses gathered around the body and began to eat. It was a substantial carcass, and so the meat would last them a couple of days. Tatu arrived too late to be part of the action, but he pushed his way to feed on the carcass anyway. Chipipi arrived with the cubs to have their first taste of meat and so the entire pride settled down for the raucous pushing, shoving, snarling and cuffing that usually accompanies lions at table.

The cubs were last to feed, but the kill was so big there was plenty left for all, and enough to feed for another day or so. These youngsters were lucky. Because the other females in the pride had left with their offspring at the time of the takeover, there were no older cubs present, so the little ones had no competition from bigger pride mates. In a pride with mixed age groups, cubs die because they are excluded from kills by the older cubs.

The Tingatinga Pride cubs, however, were doing fine. Umbu was particularly diligent. She had lost cubs in the past due to her inexperience, but now she was a model mother. Through their distinctive smells and voices, she recognised her own cubs from the other 12 newborns. She licked them often, cleaning their fur of ticks, mites and general dirt from the rough-and-tumble games, one slurp from her large and powerful tongue almost lifting them off their feet. She was not particular fond of suckling the other cubs, but if she was daydreaming they snuck in anyway and siphoned off about a third of her milk supply. But it did not really matter, because whether she had one cub or four drinking, she produced the same amount of milk anyway.

The cubs grew quickly, and it was not long before they were watching how their mothers hunted, especially if it was in the daytime, when few other predators were about. Hunting school could afford to be out in the open, but on some days the temperature soared, making the whole process a greater effort than usual.

One day the entire pride, cubs and all, was lined up along a high bank near the river. It was midday and it was hot, 30 degrees in the shade, but the pride against all expectation was contemplating a hunt. They were watching a small herd of zebra coming down to the river to drink. Almost as one, the lionesses rose and slipped down behind any vegetation they could find. They were spread out, each one creeping forward a little but keeping low to the ground every time the zebra stallions were not looking up. Slowly they each edged forwards and set their trap. When all the stallions had their heads down, the first lioness burst from cover and started the chase. The target was a young zebra, not a dependent foal, but an independent youngster. It ran as fast as its powerful legs could carry it, the stallion's cries echoing in its ears, but the lioness was keeping pace. It doubled back towards the river at just the moment a second lion came alongside. It crashed through a thicket and behind the trees, losing the big cats momentarily, but then the first lioness put on an extra turn of speed, grabbed the zebra's rump and hung on. The sheer weight of the lioness caused its rear end to buckle and it was on the ground. The lioness flipped it on its side and grabbed its throat. Two more lionesses pitched up and in a matter of minutes they started to tear the unfortunate beast apart. It was food for most of the pride.

Whether the lionesses were cooperating was a moot point. They seemed to be working together, but there were often hunts where they would simply run into a herd and scatter them. As soon as one lioness had singled out a target, the others would converge on it and sheer weight of numbers eventually brought it tumbling to the ground. They may have cooperated at the end, but at the beginning it was every lioness for herself.

Sometimes, a lioness would hunt in full view of the rest of the pride, yet none of the others would lift a paw to help; like the time all the mothers and their cubs were watching another family of zebra. Msichana broke ranks and started to stalk them. The cubs, picking up the cue, hid in some bushes, but their

mothers just sat there, making no attempt to conceal themselves. They simply watched what Msichana was doing. She
approached to about 30 metres from the zebras. They seemed
to have been distracted by something in the distance, possibly a
rival stallion, and failed to see her until the very last moment.
She bolted from cover. The stallion whinnied, and the whole
herd took off, leaving the lioness in a cloud of dust. She gave
chase for a couple of hundred metres but then stopped. She sat
panting in the heat before returning to the other lionesses, who
had still not moved. They all greeted her warmly, and then they
all lay down for the remainder of the afternoon.

Grandi and Old One Eye, meanwhile, had no cubs to look
after and so were often out and about without the rest of the
pride. While the other lionesses were being no more than
spectators to a hunt, they had been out on the plains and
looking for quarry, but the heat had beaten them and they
withdrew to a solitary tree on the top of a small mound. There
was just enough shade for the two of them, and they could look
out over the plains for any signs of activity. Old One Eye's
good eye picked up movement around an old termite mound.
She stared intently at the spot. Grandi noticed her gaze and
looked too. It was a cheetah, and she was not alone. She had
cubs with her.

Generally, other predators – cheetahs, leopards, hyenas and
jackals – are considered rivals for precious resources, and lions
are rather intolerant so they do what they are particularly good
at: they eliminate the competition. The cheetah family were safe
for the moment, though. The oppressive heat ensured that the
old lionesses stayed out of the sun, and as it reached its zenith at
midday, the air temperature on the plains rose uncomfortably
high. The rest of the Tingatinga Pride was flat out and fast
asleep under a large acacia tree some distance away, so for

cheetahs this was the safest time to be out hunting, when their adversaries were resting. Grandi and Old One Eye, however, watched as the cheetah family sheltered under a fallen tree. The punk-style, long baby hair on the back of the cubs' necks helped to camouflage them but the old lionesses could still make them out. All was quite and tranquil for a while, but then a group of warthogs approached the cheetah family.

The air shimmered in the heat of the day, and the wavy shapes of the warthogs grew increasingly larger. They saw the cheetahs but did not run; instead, they walked up aggressively, their hair bristling. They seemed to want the shade too and were intent on ousting the rival family. They trotted on, and then doubled back, but the warthog piglets were lagging behind the adults.

The cheetah mother ran out from the shade, and the warthogs took flight. They raced as fast as their little legs could carry them, but it was not fast enough. The cheetah had hardly reached full speed when she intercepted the last in line. The rest of the warthogs slowed, looked back, and then trotted on, the two surviving piglets bringing up the rear. The cheetah cubs came bounding towards their mother, ready to accept the piglet she had caught; but she had not killed it.

The cheetah mother dropped the piglet and it started to run. One of the cubs deftly tripped it with its front paw, but the piglet jumped up and tried to bite its assailant. The other cubs gathered round but they were reluctant to touch such a feisty little fellow. The piglet kept them all at bay, and then disappeared down a burrow. The cubs looked on bewildered. One minute their plaything was there, and the next minute it had gone. They searched high and low but could not find it. Their meal had inexplicably evaporated.

This habit of capturing of prey and keeping it alive was the way in which cheetah mothers educate their offspring in the gentle art of killing, and these cubs had reached the stage when they were ready to learn. Later the same day, another opportunity arose.

A small group of female gazelles wandered close to the cheetah and her cubs. The youngsters remained very still, while their mother prepared to rush one of the herd. She lay almost flat against the ground, her body bunched up like a coiled spring. Her cubs, though, were learning fast. Every time she put her head down, they followed suit, but she had seen a more vulnerable target – a female gazelle suckling a newborn fawn. The mother gazelle spotted the cheetahs and started to run, leaving her young one standing. Then it took off too, with one of the cheetah cubs breaking cover and chasing behind it. The mother cheetah overtook her offspring and accelerated to full power. She soon overran the foal, but it jinked several times, evading capture at first. An outstretched paw, however, brought it tumbling down.

The cheetah grabbed the foal by the head and carried it to her cubs. She dropped it but, as it was still alive, the foal jumped up and ran, two of the cubs in hot pursuit. Several times, the mother repositioned the foal and each time the cubs tried to bring it down. Finally, the mother killed it and, while the cubs fed, a herd of wildebeest began to gather around them. Two or three had stopped to watch. They sneezed a warning to the rest of the herd –'beware, there are predators here' – and then they turned and headed for the river.

It was then that the mother saw more sinister movements on the horizon. She watched carefully. The stocky outline was unmistakable. It was Grandi, Old One Eye and the rest of the Tingatinga Pride, and they were heading her way. She rounded up her cubs and led them away in the opposite direction, looking desperately for a safe hiding place. The lions, meanwhile, were walking slowly. The mother climbed on to an old termite mound to get a better view, and she could see they were still heading towards them. The family dived into the long grass, where they were invisible, but equally they could now not see where the lions might be.

They walked in a wide arc, hoping to navigate round the danger, but the pride had changed direction. The four cheetahs stopped abruptly. Up ahead were the distinctive outlines of the lions. They were sitting or lying, with Grandi and Old One Eye ever alert. The cheetah family stood like statues. At all costs they had to avoid any contact with the lions. The three cheetah cubs would have been killed instantly. They had to play a waiting game. It was their only hope.

Grandi stood up and walked away from the rest of the pride. One by one, several of the others followed her. They were walking directly towards the cheetah family, but surprisingly the mother ignored the lions and started to stalk a group of female Grant's gazelles. This was madness, but the urge to hunt had mysteriously overtaken her need to flee. If she brought down a gazelle the lions would be on her in an instant. Nevertheless the cheetah continued, edging increasingly nearer her quarry and seemingly oblivious to the approaching threat.

The gazelles were nervous. They had seen the lions but not the cheetah. They stood and looked anxiously about them. The cheetah broke cover and started her run but realised immediately that she had no chance to catch them and aborted the hunt, which was just as well. The lions had seen the gazelles take off and they started to trot to the spot. There were lionesses everywhere, but somehow they failed to see the cheetah mother or her cubs; instead, they were focussed on the herd of wildebeest behind her. One lioness picked her target and gave chase. It was a relatively young animal. She leaped at it from the side and brought it down in a cloud of dust.

But that was not all. Three more lionesses were trying to kill a larger wildebeest, and two others had succeeded in flooring another youngster. There was pandemonium. Wildebeest stampeded back and forth with the remaining members of the pride in hot pursuit. Three wildebeest were down, yet they were still going for more. It was an extraordinary sight. Undoubtedly the Tingatinga Pride was becoming one of the strongest and most formidable on the plains, and now they were showing it. The cheetahs, however, remained glued to the spot amongst the chaos all around them.

Mbili and Tatu, as usual, appeared when the action was over, and appropriated the largest carcass, but there was plenty for all. The pride had done well. Their table manners, though, were less auspicious. Unlike the cheetah family that was orderly at table, the lions scrapped, snarled and swiped at each other all the way through their meal. Mbili and Tatu, having taken the best meat from their own carcass, abandoned it to the cubs and muscled their way into the lionesses' food. The quarrelling went well into the night. The cheetahs left quietly while the lions fed.

CHAPTER SIX

– Unwelcome Attention –

It was early in the morning. Trees and bushes were black silhouettes against the blush of red and yellow from a sun that had still to rise. The mother cheetah jumped effortlessly on to a low termite mound, scanning the plains for any signs of food. The fur of her head glowed yellow as the sun's golden orb pushed above the horizon, turning the land and sky into fire. It was the start of another long and languid day.

An untidy flock of starlings flapped out of a flat-topped acacia and flew out over the plains. Wildebeest and zebra, silhouetted against a terracotta haze, looked up as a line of lionesses, the females of the Tingatinga Pride, sauntered across the distant horizon. They had been hunting all night, but unsuccessfully. At best, a group of lions such as these could only expect a success rate of about 30 per cent. Most often their prey gets away. Now, it was time to turn in and recharge their batteries, ready for another try. The other animals turned away, yet remained vigilant. For the moment, these lions would be no threat and somehow they knew it. Was it something in the way these predators moved, or was it some other unknown and mysterious force? Whatever the reason, the wildebeest, gazelles and zebra went back to feeding, the wildebeest grunting continuously in their characteristic way and the zebra stallions watching out for their family groups. The grass was green and moist. For many it looked to be a good day.

On a distant ridge, a line of elephants walked soberly passed a solitary, flat-topped acacia, and a small herd of gazelle ambled almost casually alongside the cheetah's three sizeable cubs, yet ready to flee at the slightest hint of danger. The cubs were the female's fourth attempt at raising a family. Other predators had killed all her cubs from previous litters, and high on the list of culprits was the Tingatinga pride.

The entire pride – adults, sub-adults and cubs – were on the move, walking along a track through the long grass. It was about three years since Mbili and Tatu had taken over and now it and the pride had grown and matured. The first litter of cubs had become troublesome adolescents, and two of the sisterhood of lionesses – Umbu and Msichana – had given birth to their second. These cubs were a little over five months old, but Chica had given birth much later than the other females, so her single male cub Kitoto was only in his second month. He was, therefore, considerably smaller than the other cubs and at a distinct disadvantage, both during play and at meal times. His older siblings batted him about endlessly but the feisty little fellow bounded back for more. His close ally was Ndugu, an underdeveloped male who was from the second litter and the runt of the group. The two cousins played together, and seemed inseparable.

The remaining pride female Chipipi was without new cubs but was becoming receptive again, and both Mbili and Tatu had taken a strong interest in her. They rarely fought, but on this occasion there was trouble brewing. Tatu was especially aggressive. He chased Mbili away, before the two squared up to each other and snarled warnings across the small gap between them. This was unexpected behaviour. The two lions were usually close allies as well as close brothers.

Kitoto, however, was his usual confident self. He waltzed straight up Chipipi and started to play, despite the close presence of the two males. They ignored him and, after a romp and some head rubbing, he returned to his cousin for something more boisterous. As the older lions sat or lay about, the mob of youngsters fooled around in the grass, the young males fighting and the female cubs honing hunting skills in games of tag and tumble. They were well fed and full of energy – signs that the pride was finding sufficient food. In fact, the pride had never been bigger – 29 lions and lionesses of all sizes.

Suddenly, all the cubs stopped their games. Mbili and Tatu had stood up. The two males were almost regal, except that their faces were covered in irritating flies. Kitoto then took a fancy to Tatu's tail. The big male turned his head and snarled, putting the little one firmly in his place. He backed off and Tatu went on his way. For the rest of the pride, it was time to move on too. There was hunting to be done. Maybe they would have more success with an early morning hunt. The mothers stood, stretched, yawned and walked. Grandi, as usual, was in the lead, with Chica and the cubs bringing up the rear.

It was not long before they came across a small group of zebra in long grass. Two lionesses dropped immediately into stalking mode, keeping low and hidden. They almost crawled towards the family party, but the stallion was fully alert. He let out the whinnying alarm call, and the zebra were alert. Something had spooked them, even though the lions had remained undetected.

Out of the long grass came Kitoto. He had walked into the open, as bold as brass, and given the game away, bringing the hunt to a grinding halt. The zebra, however, did not run. They turned to look at the youngster, now aware that there were lions about. There was no point it stalking those animals any more. The lionesses abandoned the hunt and strolled away.

Kitoto found a stream, jumped from one rock to another and slipped in. In a flurry of spray, he clambered out, soaked to the skin. Ndugu was quickly alongside him, the reassuring older cousin, and the two went off to roll in the long grass and chase about in the mud.

Without Kitoto's able assistance, one of the lionesses eventually brought down a zebra and the pride gathered at the kill site. Ndugu was quick to join the adults at table, but little Kitoto was more reluctant. He could smell the kill, but it was too strange a thing for a small cub to comprehend. His mother walked over to give him reassurance and lead him to the carcass, but still he would not go; that is, until he spotted Ndugu tucking in, and it was this more than anything else that convinced him the carcass was safe. He pushed his way through the long grass, sniffed at the meat tentatively and licked a piece. Watching Ndugu tearing at the meat, he copied him and started to chew on a piece of skin. He was batted about a bit, as is the usual with lions feeding, but he held his own. It was his first solid meal, but he would still depend on mother's milk for a long while yet.

A couple of hours later, the carcass had been demolished and most of the pride was sated, including the two young companions. Their little tummies were bulging but it did not stop them fighting. But it was time to rest, and a slap from Chica stopped Kitoto in his tracks. It was time to simmer down, time for siesta.

The entire pride was dozing. Kitoto was in the embrace of one of his aunts, but it was not long before he was up to mischief. A lion cub's favourite toy must be an adult's tail. It gives hours of fun and helps it perfect the pounce and the bite, and Kitoto was making full use of it. Each time the tail was lifted he jumped, grabbed it and wrestled it to the ground, but as soon as he bit it the patient adult waved it away and the game started all over again. And when he was tired of that, he went to annoy Ndugu, but the older cub had the last laugh. He stalked and caught the little cub, causing him to roll on his back with his little feet waving submissively in the air. Then, it was a sleeping Mbili's turn, with Kitoto rummaging through his mane, clambering on his back and sliding down his face. Mbili just pawed the air gently and went back to sleep. Kitoto changed playmate. He rather foolishly went to Tatu, and got a snarl, bared teeth and almost a cuff from his giant paw, which sent him straight back to Ndugu and a more gentle game of tag. The game, however, was interrupted.

The pride was hidden amongst the bushes of a dense thicket but, as they slumbered, an enormous herd of two or three hundred buffalo came to feed nearby. They were moving gradually towards the pride's rest site. Every now and then, one of the buffalo raised its head, licked its nose and carefully sniffed the air. They were watchful, but grazed peacefully and were quite unaware that the lions were there. A buffalo snorted and the lions woke up and were immediately alert. They looked out and saw the buffalo approaching. Such a large herd could be a danger to the cubs. Kitoto remained unusually quiet, hiding in amongst the thick stems of a bush. If the buffalo charged, he would be vulnerable. His only defence was not being seen.

Two buffalo grunted a warning and the rest raised their heads. They had spotted one of the lions. It was Kitoto. He had given the game away again, but this time it was serious. Kitoto had run out into the open to be with his companion. Now the two of them were in great danger. The buffalo lined up, looking and sniffing, while the lionesses held their ground, hidden as they were in the midst of the thicket.

The buffalo were becoming increasingly agitated and gradually more animals came to reinforce the wall of horns and hides. Kitoto's mother remained hidden in a hollow as long as she could, but a bull buffalo had broken ranks and had run around behind her. She was trapped. It came down the slope and into the hollow, its horns at the ready. The lioness climbed out quickly and ran, the buffalo on her tail, but the beast pulled up short and began thrashing the bushes. It and the other bulls were going through the undergrowth systematically, searching for any signs of lions. The rout had but a single purpose – to trample or gore to death any that they found, no matter their size.

Ndugu and Kitoto squirmed through the thick vegetation, trying to keep one step ahead of the flailing horns and trampling feet. The buffalo snorted and pushed forward. Kitoto's mistake had jeopardised the survival of them both. But while the buffalo were occupied with the two cubs, the rest of the pride made good their escape. After much trampling and thrashing, the buffalo gave up and went on their way.

A couple of hours later, Kitoto's mother returned to the spot and called. She had come back for her cub. The older cub Ndugu was already with her, but Kitoto was nowhere to be seen. They searched the bushes and long grass and then turned their attention to a rocky area with thick vegetation. They visited every slab, looking underneath and all around. A red-faced lizard with blue trousers scampered for cover, but it was in no danger. The lions had other things on their mind. They called with a muffled, low-pitched roar, and then they heard a quiet miaow coming from a pile of flat stones. There was Kitoto, alive and well. He had survived the buffalo attack. He ran out from his hiding place, but the long grass prevented him from seeing his mother, and she from seeing him. They both called urgently, and then, after a heart-stopping few minutes, they found each other. They were together again.

It was about this time that Tatu began to go AWOL. He disappeared for several days, leaving Mbili the sole defender of the pride. It was likely to put his brother and the group under tremendous pressure, for the neighbours would soon realise that the defence was weak. For the moment, though, Mbili was coping. There had been no serious incursions and the morning and evening proclamation was still delivered with gusto. First, the older lionesses roared, and Mbili joined them. Their deep, earthy chorus echoed across the land. Their message was clear: 'This is our patch, other lions keep out!' All the members of the pride took part, even little Kitoto. His little bleat was a long way from a roar, but he was learning fast that lions only rule from a position of strength and roaring at dawn and dusk was one way to advertise their might.

This time, however, it attracted unwelcome attention. A pair of nomadic males, not dissimilar to the brothers in their youth, walked into the Tingatinga Pride territory. They had nothing to lose except their dignity and perhaps a few handfuls of fur, so they just waltzed right in. Mbili confronted them at first, roared loudly in their direction, but they seemed unimpressed. He roared some more, but they kept on coming. This was not the time for token heroics, so he turned and walked, as nonchalantly as possible, in the opposite direction.

In fact, he was walking rapidly, but trying to give the appearance of not running away. The longer he could keep this up, the less likely the intruders would chase him; but they were tight-lipped, as if they were hunting, and had a fixed stare directly at this lone male who was no more than 50 metres in front of them. They were nomads, their untidy hairstyles betraying their youth, but they were tough and more than a match for a lion on his own. Mbili stopped momentarily and roared at them defiantly, but that simply set them off. They began to run. Mbili turned and ran too.

The rest of the pride, sensing the cubs were in danger, made for cover. They entered some woodland and hid. They waited there for several hours, until the nomads had gone. The older cubs were first to emerge, clambering over fallen tree trunks, intent on playing, no matter what was happening around them. The adults joined them and they climbed on to the higher boughs where they could see for some distance over the plains. The coast seemed to be clear, and their ears suddenly pricked up at the unmistakable roar of Mbili.

He had evaded the two nomads and was back on his patch, declaring his ownership. They, however, had not gone far. They were biding their time, waiting for another opportunity to test the resilience of this resident male. It was a pattern that would become all too familiar during the next few months.

The next problem, however, did not involve intruders. It was a resident that was on a collision course with the pride – a resident leopard. Her territory was on both sides of the river at the edge of the Tingatinga Pride's range. Like the lionesses, she was rearing offspring, in her case, a single male cub. She had just killed a gazelle and was leading her cub to eat, when she stopped dead. Something was wrong. She was uneasy about going any further but did not quite know why. The reason, however, was just over the other side of the river. She could not see them, but several lionesses of the Tingatinga Pride were resting between her and the carcass she had left. After a brief hesitation both leopards continued, using the high grass as a cover. They passed a lone bull elephant feeding near some low bushes, but he paid no heed to them.

Reaching the riverbank they walked along the top of the embankment heading towards their usual river crossing, but the lionesses had stirred too, so leopard and lions were converging on the same place. Overhead the sky was darkening, and large thunderheads were forming over distant hills. There was a storm coming, but there could be an even greater tumult if the lions and leopards should meet, and the leopards, especially the cub, would be worse off.

The lions made their way down to the water's edge, and the two rivals came face to face across the river. Before the lions could make it to the other side, the two leopards shinned up a tree. They were safe as long as none of the lions could climb. One of the lionesses sniffed around at the base of the trunk and looked up. The leopard bared her teeth and snarled. The lion responded with a quiet roar. She was calling in other members of the pride. Soon, the entire pride would be milling about. The leopard mother watched from on high, leading her cub to safer branches at the top of the tree. As long as the cub's nerve held and he did not try to escape from the tree, he would be fine. It was going to be a long night.

In the morning, the leopards were still in the tree with a couple of two-year old male lions patrolling its base. Eventually boredom got the better of them and they moved off. The mother leopard was able to climb down and check if the coast was clear. Rather nervously she made her way down to the river to drink. It was time to recover her kill . . . if it was still there. She had hidden it in thick vegetation, and when she reached the thicket the dead zebra foal was still in place. She took the head end, straddled the corpse, which was almost as heavy as she was, and dragged it to the nearest tall tree. Like an agile rock climber, she went up the tree and into a fork about ten metres above the ground without so much as stopping for a breath. After a brief rest, she began to tear into the meat.

Her cub was still up the tree that had been surrounded by

lions. He was a little uneasy about venturing down, but in due course hunger got the better of him and he contemplated the potentially risky journey from one tree to the other. Having made the decision, he descended and trotted quickly, but as he went up, she came down. She had eaten her fill, leaving the best part of the carcass for her offspring. She went to the river to drink, but as she reached the bank there was Grandi and Old One Eye. As soon as they spotted her, they gave chase.

The leopardess made good her escape up another fig tree. She rested across a large branch arching over the river, catching her breath and peering down at the two lionesses. They, in turn, looked up at her. One even tried to shin up the trunk. But that was the difference between leopards and lions. While lion cubs can shin up a tree, adults are not especially good climbers. The leopard walked casually back and forth along her branch, well clear of the lionesses, but she did not dare come down. These two would kill her instantly, but try as they might they could not get up the tree. It was stalemate. They went to find the rest of the pride, leaving the leopard to herself.

Almost the full contingent of the Tingatinga Pride was present on this dry, bright morning. Mbili was strutting around greeting the lionesses and cubs, including the smallest – Kitoto. The little one continued to take liberties with Mbili, but he still had to watch out for Tatu's temper or he could get a swipe that would bowl him over in the dust. The older cubs played, one biting another's tail, and two stalking each other in a game that ended inevitably in a rough-and-tumble. They were all well fed and seemingly content, but this tranquil family scene hid more sinister developments.

Tatu had been spending even more time away from the

pride, and the young nomads were still around. They were beginning to have designs on the Tingatinga Pride's territory. Mbili and his young offspring were becoming extremely vulnerable. For the moment, though, they were all together; all, that is, except Tatu again.

He was out on the plain, heading for who knows where, when he came across a mother cheetah stalking wildebeest calves. He paid little attention at first, but quickly put two and two together. If the mother was successful, there was an easy meal to be had. He stopped, lay down and waited for the action. Fortunately for the cheetah, the lion dozed off, just as she was just about to make her move.

The wildebeest were streaming through the long grass in a single line. The cheetah mother watched them go, searching their ranks for the more vulnerable youngsters. She spotted one and started her run. The target stepped out of line and made a U-turn. The cheetah leaped against it, grabbed its throat and wrestled it to the ground. It was all over in a few seconds. When the body went limp she yelped for her cubs to join her. She looked around anxiously. They were nowhere to be seen. She yelped again, and again, and then she heard their faint but familiar chirping calls. They came bouncing through the long grass, jumped all over their mother in greeting before assembling around the kill. While they all tucked in, the mother kept looking around. Satisfied that the coast was clear she began to feed too. They fed for a surprisingly long time. Normally they would wolf down as much meat as quickly as they could and then move on, but they were still in the same spot a couple of hours later. Having finished, they walked to a familiar resting site by an old termite mound.

Looking about her, however, she found that one cub was missing. She looked out anxiously over the plains but it was nowhere to be seen. Risking a confrontation with a larger predator, she led the three survivors back to the kill site in the hope that the fourth cub was somewhere nearby and hiding. She called. No answer. She went on calling. If the cub was out there somewhere, she wanted to find it. The three cubs called too. Still nothing.

By the time they reached the carcass, the bones were strewn about as if something had trashed the site and several vultures were picking through the few remaining morsels of meat. The birds moved away reluctantly, one or two launching into the air. The missing cub, however, was not there. The family walked on. The mother called again, even more urgently. Then she stopped and started sniffing around. The cubs joined her. There was something on the ground. It was the missing cub. A lion kill. Abandoned. Tatu had been this way.

By ten o'clock, with the sun rising high in the sky, the pride sought shade. A small tree surrounded by some large bushes was all the cover there was for miles around, so the lionesses and cubs squeezed together underneath its branches and relaxed. Cubs suckled and adults dozed but, even with his eyes closed, Mbili was alert for any unusual sounds or smells. After a while, he made his rounds of the trees and bushes, rubbing his head amongst the branches and spraying urine on the trunks. It was a serious business, scent-marking his territory, but the cubs that accompanied him failed to see the sobriety of the occasion and romped about in the grass. One day the males amongst them would have to scent-mark in earnest themselves, but not for now. Play was the order of the day.

The air shimmered as Mbili's wavy outline appeared on top of a mound. He looked out over the plains for any hint of intruders. He looked agitated. He had picked up the telltale signs of the rival males. They were far off for the moment, but at any time they could be on his doorstep. He had to be ready. His cubs depended on him. He walked slowly across the gently undulating grassland, his grassland . . . at least for the time being . . . putting up a large flock of cattle egrets that had been dining on insects in the grass. He ignored them. He was watching intently the distant horizon.

The females of the pride had their mind on other things. It was their job to bring in dinner and their targets were amongst a small group of resident wildebeest. They had not moved out with the migration, but were passing through, on their way to the river to drink, grazing as they went. The grass was especially long, so the lions could stalk them with little risk of being seen. Indeed, one lioness was just five metres from a wildebeest male when she started her run.

The quarry bolted, the lioness close behind. It ran in a wide arc and then turned back on itself, jinking left then right in an attempt to confuse the cat. She, in turn, followed its every move, until she stretched and dug her claws into either side of its rump, bringing its rear end crashing to the ground. She was on her own, but still managed grab its throat and bite hard, preventing the beast from breathing. With her broad nostrils, she could breath hard even with her mouth closed. She remained locked in that position while waiting for the others to join her.

The rest of the pride sauntered over surprisingly slowly, almost ambling along, not a care in the world. The other lionesses and cubs gathered round, and one by one they began to pierce the victim's hide and tear off pieces of meat. Mbili wandered over, equally slowly. He seemed to have a lot on his mind, and stopped short of the kill. It was not like him to withdraw from a feast, but that was just what he did.

A few hours later, Mbili was out in the open, some distance

from the rest of the pride. He was roaring and looking intently towards the southern boundary. There, the two strangers were looking back towards the source of the sound.

The intruders approached closely. They were just a few metres from Mbili, but this time he stood his ground. There was going to be a fight and, being alone, Mbili was at a distinct disadvantage. He stared at them and they stared back, neither party daring to make the first move. Each one alone would not stand a chance against Mbili, but the two working together had a chance of victory.

Mbili started to roar again, and pawed the ground, while the young pretenders circled. Mbili strutted towards them. He was taking the fight to them. The youngsters looked at each other, and looked back at the big male heading directly towards them. They were becoming unsure of themselves, unsure whether they had the fighting power to overcome such a magnificent beast.

Mbili stood for a moment, and then moved a few paces closer. The youngsters glanced at each other again and thought better of it. They turned slowly and walked away, careful not to cause Mbili to attack. He had won the day, and no blood had been spilt, but there would be more pretenders to his throne. If Tatu did not return soon, the pride – especially the cubs – could be in trouble, and right on cue Tatu appeared over the rise . . . but he was not alone!

A mysterious young female accompanied him. She appeared quite suddenly in front of Mbili, who was about to start some judicious scent marking, and she was not in any way reserved. She ran up to him, put her head beneath his chin and almost lifted him off the ground. She ran around him, nudged him and lay belly up in submission. Mbili was bemused. Who was she? Where had she come from? He went back to a bit of scent marking, unsure what else to do. But then she put on the same performance for Tatu, but took it that little bit further. She ran up to him, and lowered her back end to the ground. She was definitely inviting him to mate.

Each time he tried, however, she rolled away and made playful roaring sounds. The pride females picked up the stranger's calls. They stopped what they were doing and went to investigate. This pride male would have some serious explaining to do, and the young female was in danger of her life.

The lionesses arrived within minutes and gathered together a few metres away while they worked out what was going on. The youngster saw them and quickly made herself scarce, trotting at first, but when the lionesses started to run, she ran too. Mbili backed away. He was having nothing to do with the affair, but Tatu joined the young female and ran behind her. The four lionesses brought up the rear, slowing occasionally to roar their warning.

By midday, the heat slowed down the lionesses to a walk. They abandoned the chase and returned to attend to their cubs. Tatu, however, remained with his new concubine, following along a few metres behind her. With his thick mane around his neck he was really feeling the heat, but the prospect of continuing his elicit liaison overcame his desire for shade. The two rested amongst some tufts of long grass, the old boy panting heavily. He was not the lion that he once was!

Nevertheless, it must have been quite a night. Tatu and his illicit partner slept long into the day. Not even a raucous troop of monkeys disturbed them. They were dropping down from one stand of trees and hot-footing it across the savannah floor to the next when they were confronted unexpectedly with Tatu's prostrate body. They chattered noisily, calling in alarm, but he did not even twitch. There was, however, something coming that would probably wake the dead – a lone bull elephant. He was huge, by far the biggest elephant in this part of the plains, and he was heading straight for the sleeping couple. He walked slowly and deliberately. They must have felt the vibrations on the ground, for they suddenly leaped up and looked about them, somewhat bewildered. The elephant flapped his enormous ears, making him look even bigger. The two lions ran. Elephants always have right of way.

Tatu and mistress may have escaped the wrath of the elephant, but in their rush to get out of the way, they ran straight into an enormous herd of buffalo, and the herd was not at all pleased to see a couple of lions. They lined up and began to advance. Tatu trotted at first, but had to put on speed as the trickle of pursuers turned into a full-scale stampede. They chased the lions for about a kilometre, but fortunately even Tatu could keep ahead of them. As the buffalo slowed their pace and stopped, the lions disappeared over a rise and were clear of the danger. The couple would have to seek solace elsewhere.

The lioness, however, was not a nomad, but one of the younger members of the Makali Pride that lived on the other side of the river. Tatu was definitely pushing his luck, and little did he know that the new love of his life was more of a Trojan horse than a Helen of Troy. Her liaison with Tatu enabled her to look over the Tingatinga Pride's territory, and because she was with him, it lessened the likelihood of her being torn apart, even though the Tingatinga females were undoubtedly aggressive towards her. What was certain, however, was that this affair was going to end in tears.

In fact, it started slowly but it was not long before incursions from the neighbours were becoming more frequent. On one occasion, when Tatu was with the pride, he and his brother were resting near their eastern boundary, close to the river, only tens of metres away from four females from the Makali Pride.

Neither knew the other was there until one of the females spotted the brothers and approached to within 50 metres. She sat, her ears back and her head low. Tatu rose, and marched towards her. She fled and the others joined her, racing back across the river.

A few days later, Mbili flushed a Makali Pride female from a thicket in which she had hidden a Thomson's gazelle that she had just killed. He gave chase, but while he was away another female tried to abscond with the carcass. Tatu intercepted her. She dropped the animal, and Tatu appropriated the food and began to tuck in while Mbili pursued the other female. He almost caught her, but she turned and cuffed him with the claws on her forepaws, before disappearing on the other side of the river. Mbili stood and roared. Things were getting sticky, and intruding lions were not the only cause.

While the Tingatinga lionesses and cubs were resting they became surrounded again by grazing buffalo. This time, the pride was effectively trapped. The lionesses – especially the mothers – looked around anxiously. The cubs scattered, finding cover as best as they could. When the buffalo discovered the lions were there, they went on the offensive as usual. Grandi and the other older lionesses started a diversion, but the herd seemed bent on annihilating the cubs. The buffalo chased them mercilessly. Had any of them – adults and cubs alike – slipped or fallen then they would have been gored or trampled to death, and the buffalo had no respect for the environment. They crashed through bushes and pushed over small trees in their attempts to get at the lion cubs. The little ones were terrified, and the noise was deafening.

The buffalo snorted, bellowed and grunted loudly, while the lions roared and snarled. It was mayhem as the buffalo systematically ploughed through every corner of the thicket, thrashing at bushes with their flailing horns and ramming the thick black bosses on their forehead into the ground. They were surprisingly nimble, galloping around and turning this way and that. The lions dodged and squirmed, goading the buffalo into attacking them and not the cubs. Grandi leaped on to a buffalo's back and was thrown off immediately. She crashed to the ground but was on her feet instantly, provoking attack after attack, anything to stop them harming the cubs.

Eventually, the noise subsided and the buffalo drifted away. The lionesses watched them go, and then searched desperately for their offspring. The real cost of the attack was about to be revealed as the surviving cubs crawled out of their hiding places. The mothers milled about, calling in gentle, low-pitched roars. Any cub that was alive responded with little bleats and miaows. There was much head rubbing and enthusiastic reunions, but not all the cubs emerged to greet their mothers.

A mother licked her dead cub, unsure what to do. It was Kitoto. His companion Ndugu walked over and nudged his lifeless body, but Kitoto did not move. Ndugu seemed puzzled that the little cub did not play. He sniffed at the tiny corpse and batted it with his forepaw, then turned and went to find his mother. Mercifully, all of the older cubs had survived. Somehow they had cowered in ditches or behind fallen logs and evaded the horns and hooves. They were gathered together and the entire pride decanted to a small stand of acacia trees, where they remained for the best part of the day.

In the evening, when the temperature had dropped and the buffalo attack was long forgotten, it was time to find food. There was no room for grief in lion society. Life had to go on. The pride assembled. The lionesses yawned, stretched and greeted one another in the usual way. It was almost a roll call, establishing if everyone was ready to hunt. At some unknown signal, Grandi made her way out of the copse and the other lionesses followed. The cubs were left behind; they would get in the way. Ndugu remained as babysitter. It was a huge responsibility and a frustrating one. As he and the cubs gazed out over the plains, what seemed like all of East Africa's game animals trooped past. Lions that are clearly visible do not present a threat, especially a bunch of cubs, so small herds of gazelle, families of zebra and the odd resident wildebeest came to within a few metres of the crèche. Ndugu had the urge to chase them but that would have meant abandoning the cubs, and then he would be for it. He sat upright in the shade and waited for the lionesses to return. The cubs, though, had other ideas.

One by one they walked out into the open. Ndugu quickly followed, but when he felt they had gone too far, he ran to the front of the column and led them back to cover. When the lionesses returned, they came empty-handed. The hunt had failed. The cubs would go hungry. Nevertheless, they greeted their mothers with an enthusiasm fit for heroes. After much head rubbing and tail pulling they all settled down until nightfall. Any chance of sleeping and charging their batteries before the hunt was dashed, however, with a change in the weather.

The wind increased dramatically and the sky darkened. Shards of lightning could be seen above the horizon and the low grumble of thunder rolled across the plains. A few shafts of sunlight illuminated patches of grass, turning them into tiny fields of gold. Antelope and gazelles crowded together, their backs to the wind. The pride went into a huddle. All the animals were ready to ride out the coming storm.

First a few drops of rain splattered on the parched ground, sending up tiny dust clouds into the air. Then the heavens opened. Driven by the wind, the rain lashed at every living thing. It hissed and boiled, while bolts of lightning flashed all around. A fork hit a nearby tree, cleaving it into two, the noise making the entire pride jump, including Mbili. Thunder and lightning came almost simultaneously. The storm was directly overhead. Most of the pride was under cover of trees and bushes, but Ndugu remained in the open. He was drenched. His young charges had abandoned him and clustered together with their mothers.

The storm ended quickly, its dying moments marked by a rainbow that arched over distant hills. The sun reappeared, only to set again moments later. Evening was coming. The temperature had dropped; perfect conditions to go hunting. The prize, however, was no more than a warthog. Mbili showed his disdain by not coming to the supper table, but the lionesses and cubs, still bedraggled from the rain, crowded around the carcass, each trying to obtain a share. In the scrum, cubs were slapped and batted by their elders, and any that begged food from a lioness was sent away with a flea in its ear. Many of the cubs gave up altogether, preferring to seek out their mothers and drink milk instead. With the rather frugal meal quickly finished, cubs were licked clean and adults groomed their fur. The pride was ready to hunt again, this time under cover of darkness.

The night, however, was as bleak as the day had been, which meant the pride had not eaten properly for several days. Things were not looking good. And it was a chilly dawn when the two nomads entered the territory again. They wandered about almost casually. Mbili was first to spot them. Tatu, who was fortunately with the pride at the time, saw him staring into the distance and came to join him. With their heads erect and proud, they continued to observe the intruders at a distance. They would get the measure of them before they attempted to chase them out. The lionesses gathered the cubs and led them to a safe place in the marsh, while the brothers let loose with a fusillade of roars. The intruders responded in kind, but if Mbili and Tatu could intimidate these upstarts with the loudest roars, they could avoid any bloodshed. They walked confidently towards the strangers, roaring as they went, and the tactic worked. The other lions backed down and, at a slow trot, they left the area. This time they probably would not be back. The presence of two strong pride males saw to that. Mbili scent marked the place where they stood. The brothers had triumphed . . . this time. Mbili flopped down and Tatu rolled over him in a cloud of flies. Then they got to their feet and rubbed heads and shoulder-to-shoulder they marched back to the pride.

Food was becoming scarce and there were signs that a drought could envelop the land. The migration had not yet arrived and the hunting was unusually poor, but the pride would try. The lionesses got to their feet, yawned, engaged in their copious head rubbing, and stretched up to scratch the trunk of the tree under which they had been resting, before heading out on to the plains.

Their first target was close to the marsh, a lone waterbuck. He was motionless, his long body set on short, stocky legs. Lions in this region tended to target his type when other food was unavailable. Waterbuck meat and fat is oily and has a musky smell, but with nothing else to hunt it would have to do. Three of the lionesses started to stalk. They lowered their heads and glided effortlessly through the long grass. Grandi was in pole position directly in front of the waterbuck, while Old One Eye slipped around in an arc to the left and Umbu to the right. It would have been the perfect pincer movement, except that two crowned cranes came along, spotted Umbu and piped up an alarm. Animals on the plains are tuned in to one another's warning calls, so the waterbuck was ready to act. He looked about him, but the lionesses were so well hidden he could not see them. They froze until the birds had gone.

The waterbuck began to relax. It lay down on the ground. Only its massive, forwardly-curved horns were visible above the grass, his grizzled, grey coat blending in with the background. He was here because he depended on water, even less able to survive a drought than domestic cattle. Grandi began to make her move, except that Umbu was standing upright in the grass for all to see, with her tail flicking back and forth. The waterbuck spotted her immediately and sneezed his warning signal. What was she doing? Grandi continued to stalk, although the chances of bringing down this individual were almost nil. The antelope turned and ran, the two patches of white on his rump clearly visible as he fled. They would have to look for something else.

The second target was a large, male warthog sporting two long ivory tusks. He was almost invisible as he rooted around in the long grass, but Grandi had spotted him. The lionesses spread out, Grandi circling behind and her two companions moving to left and right at the front. At first, the pig failed to notice it was being stalked, but the snap of a twig gave them away. The animal was ready to run, but the lions had surrounded him. They closed in. He grunted. Grandi charged. The warthog took off, his tail carried high in the air like a marker flag. He had a tremendous turn of speed, but he ran directly into the path of Umbu. She ran parallel to him for a few metres, distracting him, and Grandi slammed into him from the other side. The warthog squealed and kicked but when Grandi grabbed its throat it was quickly subdued. The four lionesses settled down to eat. It was not a big meal, but there was some meat left over, so when Chica arrived with the cubs there was a snack for each of them. It would keep the pride going for a little while longer, at least until they were able to track down something bigger.

It was not that long before the opportunity arose. It was late afternoon. The temperature had dropped and there was rain in the air. Perfect conditions. The coming storm would distract their prey, making it more vulnerable to a concerted attack. The pickings, however, were meagre. The large herds had left the Tingatinga Pride's territory several weeks ago. All, that is, except one lone beast. He had had a huge chunk taken out of his rump, probably by a crocodile when he last crossed a river, and was limping badly. The lionesses saw him and two of them sauntered across the plain towards him, contemplating an easy kill. The wildebeest had other ideas. He was still full of life and was not going to let an injury stop him from putting up a fight.

The rain was still falling when the first lioness came to within a few metres of their quarry. She started to run and the wildebeest took off. She caught up with him in seconds, but was confronted not with a rump but with the animal's front end. He charged and the lioness jumped back just as a second lioness came around from behind. The wildebeest twisted around to charge her too, but the first cat was already flying through the air. She slammed into his side, toppling him and she was at his throat in seconds.

First to arrive at the kill were some of the older cubs. They joined the two hunters, but they had to wait a while before they could eat. They approached nervously. The wildebeest's legs were still kicking. They had to be careful. Even now the beast could do some damage, even get back on its feet. The lioness, though, was tight on its throat and gradually its life drained away. The cubs found the wound, the perfect place to start. The other lionesses in the pride arrived in ones and twos in the driving rain. It would be the last easy kill of the migration season, so they had to make the most of it.

By three o'clock in the afternoon the rain began to ease off. The pride had eaten a large part of the wildebeest and was sleeping. Tatu, however, had ensured that what remained belonged to him. He lifted it up and carried it through the grass to hide it below a large bush. He snacked on throughout the day, snarling at other members of the pride should they come too close, but most of them were flat out in the shade, enjoying a siesta on full tummies. On the horizon, a perfect rainbow arched across the sky, and the dark clouds gave way to a bright blue sky. From horizon to horizon there were very few animals visible. Six weeks earlier it had been packed with wildebeest, zebra and gazelles. There were a few small, resident herds remaining that had not followed the annual migration but, in the main, for the Tingatinga Pride and their neighbours, the task of finding food would present them with a new and often dangerous challenge.

CHAPTER SEVEN

– Drought but No Disaster –

The sky was clear but the air damp, so a thin, early-morning mist filtered the rays of the sun. It bathed the entire landscape in a golden glow. Crowned cranes trumpeted a greeting to the new day, while all around stark white cattle egrets, like tiny ghosts, were in the shadow of great brown shapes – a large herd of buffalo. After the migration had left, they were by far the most numerous animals around. They were on the far side of a marsh by the river, scattered about in small groups, mothers with calves here and a huddle of excitable bachelors there, each unit composed either of close family or loose coalitions of unrelated animals. All was serene, apart from low mumblings as the animals grazed. The only disturbance was from a large and formidable bull who broadcast his importance by thrashing his horns against a thicket of acacia, but who spoiled the whole effect by walking away with his head adorned in a tangle of dead twigs and leaves like a frenzied scarecrow. Nevertheless, the younger bulls stayed well clear. He was the boss around here, and every buffalo knew it.

Oxpeckers darted amongst the grazers, perched on backs and heads, eagerly inspecting ears and folds in the buffalos' thick hides and deftly removing parasites and dead skin. A wrong move and a peck in a painful place prompted a host to shake its head violently, sending a thick cloud of irritating flies into the air. Every so often, a buffalo looked up and then smelled the air, searching for the telltale odour that would announce the arrival of predators.

A coqui francolin picked ticks delicately from grass stems and a pair of yellow-throated long claws, like yellow-and-black breasted jewels, pecked at seeds before flying away to an acacia tree. Several young bulls in a small bachelor group rubbed their horns against its trunk, while others sparred. One approached another with his horns down and then waited until the other did the same. With a twisting of the head and a dull thump, they clashed briefly and then parted, shuffling away as if embarrassed at having drawn attention to themselves.

And as a pair of ground hornbills boomed a duet to celebrate its 50th year, one by one, the buffalo flopped to the ground. They had eaten their fill and it was time to chew the cud, like all cattle do. Some gathered tightly together, a few lying on their sides, and always one or two with their heads erect but their eyes tightly closed. The cattle egrets busied about the recumbent bodies, impatient for the buffalo to get to their feet once more and stir up insects in the grass. The oxpeckers continued to peck and pick at anything that took their fancy, a stationary host easier to service than a mobile one.

Then – a sudden stillness. A head rose. A nose twitched. A tongue licked that nose, adding wetness to trap more odours. Other heads rose. Suddenly, the entire herd was on its feet. The smell of danger was in the air . . . lions! They could not see them but they could smell them. The mist still clung to the ground, and everything little over a metre high could move around without being seen. Only their ears were visible, but they were some distance away, on the other side of the river.

The buffalo arranged themselves in line abreast, a formidable wall of beef and horns. They stood and stared, as the pride came into view. The cats ambled down to the water's edge, stopped and looked up. On the far bank, buffalo stared back. One – the large bull – stepped forward and gave an explosive snort, a warning not to come any closer. The pride ignored the threat and walked into the river. These were cats unafraid of water, unafraid of buffalo. They waded in, up to their bellies. The herd was unimpressed.

The pride passed an eerie white buffalo skull, clearly visible in the brown, slow-moving water. They had killed here before. The buffalo stamped their feet and snorted, but still they did not run. The lions pressed on and, at an invisible signal, they started to run. The splashes spooked the herd, and they all turned almost as one . . . and *then* they ran. The ground shook with the thundering of hooves. As Mbili and Tatu appeared on the other bank, five of the lionesses raced out of the water and were quickly in amongst the buffalo. They had no target. They were testing the market, looking for signs of a limp, hobble, indecision, or a vulnerable young calf isolated from its mother.

At first Grandi, as usual, made the running, but when the rest of the pride caught up with her they fanned out and pushed the herd ahead of them. By keeping the buffalo moving there was less chance of a confrontation. Nevertheless, some of the back markers began to slow and turn, ready to make a stand, but Grandi kept on running. She had spotted a calf with its mother. If she could get between the two, in the confusion of the stampede she might separate them. A few more paces and she achieved her goal. A carefully placed cuff from her outstretched front paw brought the calf down, and she grabbed it by the head.

The mother continued with the herd at first, but quickly sensed her calf was missing. She doubled back and came thundering down on Grandi. She slammed the boss of her horns into Grandi's side, but the old cat hung on, continuing to grip the calf's head and swivelling her body away from its mother. The calf fell, but the mother, straddling her offspring, stamped on the cat with her front hooves before lowering her horns to hook them under Grandi's body, throwing her forcibly a metre or so into the air. With the wind knocked out of her, she withdrew and the calf got to its feet. The mother charged again, but her isolation from the rest of the herd meant that the cats abandoned the calf, and surrounded the mother.

She bellowed and snorted, more with frustration than anger. The cats were keeping well clear of her flailing horns and focussed on her rear end. First one then another sunk their claws into her thick skin, and held on momentarily before being flung off each time the cow whirled around. Then they were on her. One leapt on to her back, another hung around her neck and the rest dealt with the rump and hind legs. The cow stood very still, her feet spaced widely apart, and even with the sheer weight of lions, she failed to topple. Normally buffalo cows are killed in minutes, unlike the bulls that can put up a fight for hours, but this female was tougher than most. It was not over yet.

The cow bellowed, more a scream than a bellow. The herd stopped instantaneously and turned. Fleeing tails were replaced by down-turned horns. Retreat turned into an advance. They pressed forward shoulder-to-shoulder, walking slowly but steadily like an army, directly towards their herd mate and her attendant lions.

A small group of young bulls took the initiative and charged, but were brought up short by a battery of snarls and growls. The buffalo stamped their feet, smelled the air and snorted. The lionesses, their ears pinned back, bared their teeth and snarled. It was deadlock – the immobile cow, the lions guarding their prize and the rescuers uncertain of what to do next. A lunge from a young lioness provoked another charge. Two of the lionesses released their grip and made a run for it, while the third was reluctant to let go. At the last minute, she ran, horns and hooves slicing through the air around her. The young female buffalo was battered but made off and ran in amongst her herd mates.

While the rest of the herd confronted most of the other lionesses in the pride, Grandi was able to run around unseen behind them. She spotted the calf again and ran towards it. Such was her surprise attack that there was sudden pandemonium. The calf ran, but the wily old lioness brought it down. Clouds of dust billowed about them all and, as it drifted away, there were the buffalo, standing, heads up, sniffing the air, trying to make sense of what had happened.

The other lionesses caught up with Grandi, and tore into the kicking and screaming calf. The bulls in the herd heard its cries and, once they had located the sound, they came running. They bore down on the lionesses, but one by one the cats lost their nerve. The calf stood. It was dazed, but still alive, and like its mother badly mauled. While the young bulls chased the lions, the cows came around, sniffing and licking the little one, but the lions returned time and again, knocking it off its feet . . . once, twice, three times. It was not long for this world.

Eventually, the herd broke into a run and left the calf to the lions. Then they disappeared over the rise, where they stopped, spread out and started to graze as if nothing untoward had happened. The cattle egrets and oxpeckers that had been startled by the attack returned to their hosts and went about their business, while on the other side of the hill, the lionesses tucked into their meal uninterrupted, aside from an inquisitive jackal that nipped in and stole a morsel before any of the pride even noticed. Mbili and Tatu remained on the other side of the river. They would eat another time. They slept. Not long afterwards the lionesses, each replete with a bellyful of tender buffalo veal, lay down where they had eaten. They were no more than a couple of hundred metres from the herd, but a truce had been called.

The following day, as the afternoon siesta was drawing to a close, the lionesses and their offspring were still at the kill site. They rose and stretched on their side of the hill, while the buffalo were beginning to stand up on the other. Mbili and Tatu walked down to the river. They looked at the water, reluctant to get their feet wet, but all the food seemed to be on the other side. It was not all plain sailing, however. The pride had overstepped its boundary and was trespassing on the neighbours' patch. Mbili roared, followed by Tatu, just to check, but there were no answers. The lionesses pricked up their ears, but the buffalo ignored the calls. It was not their dispute. The two males took a few tentative steps into the river, and then waded slowly across. They shook the water from their manes and trotted over to the lionesses. They were greeted with a barrage of head and body rubbing, after which the brothers flopped down again, while the lionesses stood and listened.

Grandi led the way as usual, and the others followed in a single line. Up the slope they went and stopped at the top of the rise. A thin acacia thicket stood between them and the herd, but it was enough to provide them with cover. The buffalo were feeding, unaware of the visitors at first, but then they all raised their heads together, each with its nose in the air. The pride were downwind of their prey and their unmistakable smell had given them away. Without the element of surprise, again the lionesses were forced to panic the herd.

The buffalo, though, simply turned and began to put some distance between themselves and the thicket behind which the lionesses were hiding. They were in no hurry. As they ambled away, the dust rose like a smokescreen to cover their dignified withdrawal. But before they even had time to look around, the lionesses were already in amongst them. *Now* they panicked.

Lions seemed to be everywhere. The herd bunched into tighter groups. They snorted, but kept running, breaking into a gallop. Thick, brown dust was everywhere. Predators and prey were running virtually blind. Avoiding the chaos, two lionesses ran around the herd, and pulled ahead of the front-runners. They turned abruptly and were heading straight for the oncoming buffalo. The herd split down the middle, but one youngster made a wrong turn; his mother went one way, while he went the other.

Gradually, the panic subsided, and the buffalo stopped, swivelled round and confronted their aggressors. The two groups were isolated, but each still contained more than 100 animals. Now there were two impregnable walls of black, glossy head bosses and menacing horns. The cats regrouped, but a young bull broke ranks and was suddenly in their midst, his head swinging from side to side and his horn lifted in a swift upward thrust that could have skewered a lioness. The pride counter-attacked, outflanking the bull and it quickly retreated, melting back into the wall. Just then, a female buffalo ran from one group to the next. She could hear the bleating of her calf hidden amongst the feet and legs of the opposite group, and was determined to be reunited. It was what the lionesses had been waiting for. She was surrounded immediately, and they were biting at her rump and back legs, but staying well clear of her flailing horns. One lioness jumped on to her back, and the buffalo toppled over. The rest of the herd did not move. For several long minutes, they just watched the events unfolding in front of them, until another brave soul stepped forward – another bull, but older and larger this time. He strutted towards the unfortunate cow and her tormentors, his head held high at first but, as he broke into a trot, his head and horns came down into the attack position. At this signal, the rest of the buffalo began to advance too, the two separated herds slowly coalescing to form one again.

The lions, sensing the danger, abandoned the cow and stood together in front of the advancing buffalo. They snarled and growled, their ears pinned back and their canines on show, a formidable fighting group, but they could not defend their prey in the face of such overwhelming odds. The buffalo trotted closer, bellowing and grunting, and their stricken comrade hauled herself to her feet. The cats scattered as many horns sliced through the air and sharp hooves pounded the ground, but not before Grandi bit into the cow's hind leg, bringing it crashing down; but again the buffalo struggled to her feet, and between the slashing horns, again the lionesses brought her down.

The buffalo gathered around the cow. They sniffed and snorted, checking for signs of life, but she was exhausted and failed to get up. The others stood their ground. Sensing they had the advantage, they charged the lions once more, and kept on coming. The pride fled, but Grandi had not lost sight of their prize. She cleverly led the pride and the chasing buffalo in a large circle, which ended up where they began.

The injured buffalo still lay on the ground, guarded by a group of young bulls that had not followed Grandi's procession.

However, it looked as if her end was near. All the lionesses had to do was wait for the herd to disperse and, after about an hour this was, indeed, what happened. But there was still a spark of life in the wounded cow.

Seeing the herd depart, she struggled to stand, and some of the bulls turned and then gathered around her, as if they were willing her to rejoin them. She staggered a few paces, but the lionesses had already burst into action. Grandi jumped on her back, and sunk her teeth into the thick hide on the back of the buffalo's neck. The cow fell, blood streaming from another gash in her rump. She was barely alive, but the bulls tried to push their way through the hissing and snarling lionesses. An upward flick of a horn missed Grandi by centimetres, and she drew back. The lions were at risk of being gored or trampled, but they did not let up. Time and again, they piled into the dying buffalo, and time and again it struggled to rise, bellowing loudly.

All the while the two pride males had been resting some way away, back toward the river. So far, they had failed to lend a hand. The lionesses were doing all the work as usual and taking all the risks. Tatu, though, was becoming impatient. He stood and looked in the direction of the mêlée. Vultures had begun to gather overhead, a sure sign that a kill had been made, or one was imminent. Mbili rose too, and the two wandered non-chalantly through a patch of long grass towards the sounds of snarling and bellowing. With the expectation of a large and juicy steak, they emerged into the open only to find themselves in no-man's-land, the large herd of buffalo to their right and the lionesses and a group of snorting bulls to the left. They hesitated. Then Tatu, head held high and mane flowing in the wind, trotted straight towards the herd. His audacity paid off: they turned as one and fled for a couple of hundred metres, then stopped, and turned back.

At the same time, Mbili sidled up to the young bulls that had been defending the now very dead cow. They stood for a moment, and then they too turned and ran. The lionesses tore into the carcass, and the vultures began to land on the ground around them, though always making sure they kept a respectful distance. One tried to sneak a piece of buffalo meat, but Grandi cuffed it with a lightning strike of her front paw and the unfortunate bird, crippled and unable to take-off, scampered away. A wily jackal spotted the opportunity, grabbed the bird, and was away into the bushes where it could eat without being disturbed.

But others had seen the vultures too. A cacophony of unmistakable whooping announced the arrival of an untidy bunch of lolloping, thick-necked hyenas. It was Kikuto and her clan of cackling cohorts. The clan had grown big. It is said generally that four hyenas are a match for a single lion, and this group was certainly in contention for the buffalo carcass. The two sides squared up to each other, the lions hissing and growling between mouthfuls, the hyenas walking back and forth, their lunges being met with a barrage of growls. Half-a-dozen hyenas, led by Kikuto, banded together and thrust towards the carcass, their faces set in a threatening grimace, teeth bared, and their stubby, brush-like tails held erect. The lionesses sensed they could be losing their prey and ate all the quicker. The whoop calls brought in others from all around, and soon 30 or so hyenas were ready for a fight. But they had reckoned without the two pride males.

Mbili and Tatu had been chasing the buffalo, making sure they did not return in a hurry. When he saw the hyena, Tatu flipped. All the venom boiled to the surface and he exploded. He tore into the clan, seized a hyena by the head and crushed its skull. Mbili chased another, and bit it hard on the rump before upending another with his outstretched paw. He leapt on the sprawling creature, and throttled it. The hyenas withdrew rapidly, Mbili and Tatu in close pursuit, but their leader got away. That was something for another day.

On returning to the pride, Tatu rushed in and straddled the buffalo carcass. Mbili joined him and, in flurry of whirling paws and angry growls, the two males took over the meal. As usual, the lionesses would have to wait.

At midnight, Mbili woke up with a start. A lion had roared and it was not far off. Tatu was alert immediately and roared back. The resident pride was returning to the western part of its range, and the trespassers would be at a distinct disadvantage. Large though their pride had become, Mbili and Tatu were only two males to the neighbours' three. The odds were not stacked in their favour. They made their way quickly back to the river.

Grandi and others had heard the roar, and they too hurried to the river crossing, but suddenly the three resident males walked out from behind an acacia thicket and they were ready for trouble. The females froze momentarily before letting rip with a barrage of snarls. They stood shoulder-to-shoulder ready for an attack, but none came. The three lions simply lay down and paid no attention to the cowering females as if they were not there at all. They were flirting!

Blissfully unaware of what was happening to their pride females, Mbili and Tatu re-crossed the river and were back in their own territory. When they reached the home bank, they turned and roared. The rival lions immediately leapt to their feet and, with an extraordinary barrage of sound, they roared back. It was the cue for the females to make a dash for it. They slunk away, slowly at first so as not to goad the lions into an attack, and then more rapidly behind the cover of an area of tall grass. They moved low and fast, just as they do when hunting. When they found Mbili and Tatu, they joined the roaring contest, so the duet became a chorus. The three males did not follow. They stayed on their side of the river and roared back. Then all went quiet. A costly fight had been averted.

Almost all the land was coloured dusty brown. Although there was some moisture in the air to give early morning mists, it had not rained properly for months. The rains were due but only showers had fallen locally, and the buffalo, like all the large plant-eaters, had to keep moving to locate the untidy patches of green. They would be in the pride's territory for only a few days, so Grandi and the other lionesses had to make the best of it while they were there. A mature buffalo is the equivalent of two zebra or three wildebeest so hunting them, though risky, was a viable alternative to the animals of the migration. It was that or the occasional warthog.

The buffalo were grazing on one of those green patches, when a chocolate-brown calf wandered through the herd. It was bleating loudly. Every time it approached another buffalo it was kicked, nudged or head-butted, firmly rejected; after all, it was time to graze and nothing interrupted a buffalo's meal . . . except, of course, lions. The pride watched intently from a nearby knoll. The lionesses were lined up along the rise, carefully sizing up the next meal, an easy kill maybe. The calf was causing quite a stir, drawing unwanted attention to itself as it went from adult to adult in a futile attempt to find its mother. It was an orphan. The pride had made sure of that. They had killed its mother and now they were taking an interest in her calf. but how would they winkle out such an easy target from the rest of the herd?

Mbili and Tatu continued to sleep. They had no interest in the events about to unfold; at least, not yet. Grandi got to her feet. It was time for the females of the pride to go to work. The other lionesses followed Grandi's example. They stretched, yawned, rubbed heads and then stared at the grazing buffalo. The calf was still visible even though the light was fading, but it was right in the centre of the herd, in the least accessible place. Grandi led the way, and one by one the other lionesses followed in a single file behind her. The youngsters – the sub-adult males and females – brought up the rear. Mbili and Tatu did not move, and had not even noticed that the rest of the pride had gone.

The lionesses walked casually down the slope in full view of the buffalo herd. One or two animals raised their heads, sniffed the air, but then continued to graze. All was fine as long as they could see the lions. The lions, in turn, did not conceal themselves. They needed to be much closer to their target before they started to hunt. Grandi stopped. The others stood or sat on their haunches alongside her, but one of the young females could not contain her enthusiasm. She lowered her head, flattened her ears against her head and moved off low and fast across the plain. She was in danger of giving the game away. The others remained frozen to the spot. Fortunately, the land dropped away, so the buffalo could not see her, and in the twilight she was no more than a shadow in the grass.

But her inexperience showed. She appeared above the rise a shade too early. All the buffalo looked up immediately. Something was afoot. They spotted the young lioness, but instead of running away they began to trot straight towards her; two hundred gleaming, black horns, and all heading in her direction. The rest the pride watched but at first they did not move. The young lioness would learn by her own mistakes. They were more interested in the fate of the orphan calf. It was running with the herd but well hidden behind the moving wall of bodies.

Suddenly, Grandi spotted the calf. The cat's movement was almost imperceptible, but enough to alert the others that it was time to get up and go. They were on their feet and ready to run in an instant. In the meantime, the young lioness was leading the herd a merry dance. She ran across the plain at right angles to the pride and, as the flanking animals drew alongside, Grandi started to run. The other lions took off at high speed, all focussed on the calf. The nearest buffalo saw them coming. They stopped abruptly and turned, snorting and pawing the ground. The change of direction filtered quickly through the entire herd, which meant the pride, and not the young lioness, became the focus of attention.

Grandi, though, ran up to a large bull, almost taunting him to chase her. The others hissed and snarled but the buffalo were steadfast; that is, until the young lioness reappeared alongside her pride mates, and the herd recognised her. They charged. The lionesses and younger cats scattered. Buffalo and lions were running in all directions. Once again, it was just the chaos they needed.

Grandi ran, carefully negotiating her way between the huge bodies and flailing horns. Somewhere in the mêlée the calf would be defenceless, spurned by its own kind, but sought out by the pride. Grandi jinked to one side, narrowly avoiding an old bull who seemed to be relishing the altercation. As the younger buffalo ran this way and that, encouraged and manoeuvred somewhat by the cats, he stood solidly in the midst of the battle, waving his head from side to side in the bleak hope of impaling a lioness . . . or anything else that happened to be passing!

Grandi, meanwhile, had spotted the calf. Even though darkness was beginning to cast a veil over the land, her keen night vision enabled her to see what she needed. She rushed the target, leaping on to the calf's back and knocking it over. As the two crashed to the ground, another lioness grabbed the calf's throat before it could call out, and a third cat bit into a hind leg. Grandi was on her feet instantly and covered the calf's mouth and nose. Within a few minutes it was dead.

The herd began to settle down. The front rank of buffalo stood off about 100 metres away, panting, snorting and smelling the air. A small group charged forward to drive the cats back, but Grandi and her pride mates simply gave way. They already had their prize. All they had to do was wait until the herd dispersed. Mbili and Tatu, meanwhile, were where the lionesses had left them. They had missed the excitement, and there was a good chance, for the females at least, that they would also miss the meal.

Several days later, the buffalo herd crossed and re-crossed the river and were milling about within the Tingatinga Pride's territory again. Their skill at bringing down these large beasts meant that the cats had been eating well, despite the lack of rain and the absence of the migration, and they were not going to let up now. The lionesses started to walk slowly but boldly towards the wall of animals, the movement causing the buffalo to turn tail and run. The cats broke into a trot, two of the five females and a handful of youngsters running after the back markers, and three others starting to gallop in an attempt to circumvent the herd. They were manoeuvring the buffalo like sheepdogs with sheep, but somehow they had to get ahead of the stampede. They had to head off the herd before it reached the river and crossed back into the Makali Pride's territory.

The flanking females pulled up. They had run as far and as fast as they could and, besides, the first of the buffalo had reached the riverbank. But instead of plunging in and racing across, the buffalo ground to a halt. They turned and stood ready to confront the lions. The herd was still more than 200 strong, but at first only a few broke ranks and charged the five females and the handful of young lions. The pride simply fell back. They seemed to be encouraging the buffalo to chase them, anything to keep them from crossing the river. At the same time they watched for the vulnerable. Somehow, they had also to turn the manoeuvre into a hunt

The lions stopped, and the small group of buffalo pursuing them came to a standstill too. Both sides stared intently at the other, the buffalo swinging their heads from side to side and the lionesses standing tall, each with her head held high, lips pulled back and teeth very much in evidence. It was a threat display normally reserved for other lions and hyenas, but it certainly intimidated the buffalo. As the lionesses lunged forward, they retreated back into the wall, and the entire herd turned back towards the river. The tactic had failed. They were going to escape. The buffalo crashed into the water. A family of spur-winged geese – the largest goose-like bird in the world and a close relative of the shelduck – was caught unawares and forced to scatter, each bird flapping madly for the reeds on the far bank.

The lionesses lowered their heads, put their ears back and ran. They were hunting now. When a herd panics, animals make mistakes and lions can take advantage of this. As the waves of buffalo plunged into the river and waded across the relatively shallow water, a calf lost its balance and was under in a second. Grandi spotted the error and, without due regard for the alien environment, raced in to grab it. The rest of the herd crashed around her, their sharp hooves only centimetres from her head.

But, she was too late. There were Nile crocodiles in this part of the river and one had braved the mêlée. It grabbed the calf by the leg, hauled it into deeper water, and held it under. In a few minutes it was dead – drowned. Grandi could do nothing. She came back out of the water and shook herself.

Grandi refocussed. The crocodiles were keeping to deeper water, but if the pride were to pursue the herd across the river, they would have to intrude on the neighbour's land once more, and that could be dangerous. She sat down on the near bank and watched as the buffalo gradually slowed and spread out across the plain on the other side. They soon started to graze. Grandi's surveillance turned eventually into slumber, and when Mbili and Tatu came to lay down with them, the entire pride was fast asleep again.

By evening most of the herd had moved off, leaving a few scattered groups behind. In amongst them was an old bull buffalo. He was still lying down, even though the others had got to their feet and were grazing nearby. Grandi spotted him immediately. Any animal that behaves slightly differently to the others is a prime target. Seeing Grandi's purposeful stare, the other lionesses were alert too. Even the two pride males took an interest. There was plenty of meat on that old boy. Mbili licked is lips involuntarily, and pawed the ground with his hind claws. After the usual bout of heading rubbing, the pride was ready.

First, they had to cross the river without disturbing the buffalo or attracting the crocodiles. They waded gently into the shallow water and waded silently to the other side. Before they climbed the bank, they shook and then marched on. At the top of the embankment they began to stalk, trying to get as close as they could to the reclining bull before he had time to get up. All five lionesses fanned out and approached him from a small valley, so the other buffalo would not see them. The youngsters stayed back. This was dangerous work. They were too inexperienced to tackle a fully grown bull.

As they closed in on him, some sixth sense told him that something was wrong. He tried to rise, but it was too late. Just as he got to his feet a lioness slammed into his side and grabbed the back of his neck. Two others attacked his hind legs in an attempt to hamstring him. He teetered momentarily, then toppled on to his side and was quickly flipped on to his back, his legs kicking. He bellowed loudly.

At this, any of the herd within earshot came running. Two young bulls and an elderly cow approached cautiously. They held their heads high and licked their nostrils. They could smell death. One by one the herd began to form up in front of the stricken bull and the snarling cats. Every time the bull groaned, they stepped a pace forward, eager to be part of the rescue. The lions dropped back. Another large bull hooked his horns under those of the old boy and hoisted him to his feet. He staggered back to a small group, and they gathered around him, licking the blood from his wounds. Blood is salty and buffalo like to lick salt, but their guard was down and the lions were making a comeback. They rushed at the old bull, knocking him down again. The largest bull led a counter-attack, enabling the old timer to stagger to his feet again. His lip was torn, blood poured from gashes on his rump, and he could barely stand, but then the leading bull did the strangest thing: instead of attacking the lions, he slammed into the old bull, then mounted him, licked him, and smashed into him again, until he fell over. This time he failed to get up. It was as if the younger bull's patience had been sorely tested and enough was enough; it was time to move on. As he lay on the ground, he butted the old bull one more time, then turned and left, the rest of the herd following close behind.

The pride took full advantage of the lull, and raced in to claim the body. Grandi placed her mouth over his nose and mouth, while others tore into the softer skin on the belly. Mbili and Tatu had been watching the whole event from the sidelines. Only when the hunt was over did they make themselves known, commandeering the carcass and obtaining the choicest cuts; but this time the animal was so big, the two males tolerated the lionesses at the kill. They all pushed, shoved, snarled, slapped and growled until they were settled, but the youngsters had to wait until the adults had finished.

With their bellies full to overflowing, the pride slept all night beside the remains of the buffalo. A jackal ran in amongst the slumbering lions and grabbed what he could, and at sunrise the first of the vultures had begun to circle, ready to drop down and feed on the rest. The resident pride had not yet made an appearance, not so much as a roar, so there seemed to be no hurry to return across the river.

Mbili and Tatu were first to rise. They rubbed heads several times, walked leisurely to the water, and crossed without incident. The females began to do the same, but lionesses from the Makali Pride made a sudden appearance on the rise. Seeing the neighbours on their patch and the remains of the buffalo carcass, they roared first, then approached, their hair bristling, lips pulled firmly back and canine teeth exposed. The intruders backed away, hoping to escape without a fight, but the residents were having none of it. They attacked, biting and scratching several of the sub-adults on their rumps and faces. The poor creatures were surrounded, and were taking quite a beating, when Grandi stepped in. She tore into the other females, and her attack encouraged the other lionesses to join in. It was now a full-scale war, with fur literally flying and blood beginning to be shed.

Mbili heard the commotion and, realising what was happening, raced back across the river, up the embankment and into the attack. Tatu followed close behind. The resident females ran. Male lions, with their huge muscular heads and vice-like jaws, are formidable in a scrap. Mbili and Tatu, however, together with the rest of the pride were not hanging around. They did not pursue the other females. Instead, they made it quickly back to the river, crossed again safely, and ran deep into their own territory. In a turf war with their powerful neighbours, the better part of valour, as Shakespeare's Falstaff once said, is discretion, and the better part would save their lives. They regrouped, settled down and the lionesses licked their wounds.

Dry dusty days were followed by more of the same. Dust devils, whisked up by the wind, went scurrying across the parched ground. The grass, or what was left of it, was like straw, and bushes were tinder dry. Wild fires swept across great swathes of the plains, the smoke engulfing hills and valleys alike. It was December and the rains were already several weeks late. Pools were beginning to dry up, and many smaller rivers were reduced to a trickle of interconnecting ponds. The river on the pride's eastern boundary was still flowing, fed by rains that had fallen in the mountains to the far north-east. The migration was still many kilometres to the south, on the short grass plains.

Some rain had fallen locally, drawing the migrating herds southwards with the promise of a fresh green sward, but the few shoots that did grow were consumed almost as they appeared above the ground. The herds were waiting for more rain to fall and the grass to grow, but the skies were powder blue and almost cloudless. Only the smoke from wild fires, which swept across great swathes of the plains, blotted out the relentless sun.

The lions hid from the heat of the day by resting under a flat-topped acacia tree. They have fewer sweat glands than other creatures, so they panted to keep cool, their panting synchronised to their breathing – up to 200 times a minute. As they slept, a solitary buffalo chanced along. It was on its way to the river, where there was still water to be had. The pride, however, was between him and the water. This would have been an easy kill. It stood stock still, seemingly sizing up the situation. The lions, though, were unaware that he was there and continued to sleep. There was only one thing for it. The buffalo lowered its head and charged. The lions awoke with a start, and scattered in panic. The buffalo slowed and then sauntered with its head held high in the direction of the river. The pride did not attack, but returned to the tree where they all promptly lay down again. The tree, however, was not the best they could have chosen. They were sleeping on the main thoroughfare to the river, the only water for miles around, and it was rush hour.

A stark trumpeting announced the arrival of elephants. When they saw the lions they began to kick up a ruckus, hoping the lions would move on. Mbili raised his head, along with one or two of the others, but they ignored the intrusion and lay back down again. The matriarch was incensed. She grabbed a small tree, uprooted it and brandished it about, a clear sign that she meant business. She immediately had the pride's undivided attention. After a few snarls of irritation, the lions reluctantly moved away, and the elephants carried on towards the river.

Not having learned the error of their ways, the pride waited for the elephants to clear the area, then returned once more to the tree. It was not the only tree under which they could have sheltered, but for some reason they preferred that location, maybe because it now smelled comfortably of lions.

The next visitor was a rhino and calf. The mother was understandably anxious when faced with the sleeping pride. She gave the tree a wide berth, guiding her youngster quietly around the hazard . . . but the calf sneezed and it woke the lions. Mbili raised his head, saw the calf, and stood. Several of the others spotted it too. He first walked then trotted over to the rhino mother. Her calf dashed to her side and she put herself between it and the lion. Meanwhile, two lionesses and one of the young male lions crept around behind her. She spotted them and turned with unexpected agility, her horn ready to skewer any lion that should try to attack. Mbili then walked casually to and fro in front of her, drawing her attention to him rather than the others. If he could get her to attack him, the others might have a chance at bringing down the calf. But she was having none of it. Each time the lionesses made a move, the mother spun around. Mbili tried to distract her again, but the rhino was not fooled. Eventually the pride gave up and returned to their tree. It was too hot. Better to wait for sundown before they hunted again.

It was then that they heard distant voices, whistles and bells. The pride leapt to their feet. Humans! Herdsmen with their cattle had joined the procession to the river. They had no fear of the lions. Indeed, the lions had more to fear from them. Humans are dangerous. In days gone by, there were rich men with guns, and prime male lions, with their fine golden manes, were their trophies. Now, there were poor men, eking a living from the land, but this land could be cruel and unforgiving.

At one time these folk were nomadic and in harmony with their land. There were no fences, no national parks and abundant game. Echoing nature and the wild herds that follow the great migration, these proud and noble people moved their cattle with the rains. They once lived in *enkangs* – houses made of wattle and cow dung – that were abandoned when they moved on, but which were far from being blots on the landscape. The houses simply broke down and decomposed, to become part of the land once more. Nowadays, more permanent huts with thatched or corrugated tin roofs littered the edge of the wild places and, when times were hard, these people and their cattle had to compete with the wild things for the precious resources.

Livestock meant everything to these people, more so than land. It was how a man calculated his wealth, and it was the price he paid for his bride. Without cattle he was nothing. He would be destitute. But when times were hard, lions sometimes took livestock. Cattle were easy prey, but the miscreant would pay with his life. So, when people were about, the Tingatinga lions made themselves scarce. Now, there was a party heading for the river, and the pride was in the way. It was time to hide.

Grandi led the way, while Mbili and Tatu brought up the rear. As the pride melted into the vegetation, the sound of cowbells grew ominously near. The herdsmen knew the lions were there, somewhere. Each man and youth was armed with a sword-like knife or a traditional spear, the owner's single most valued possession after cattle. The spear's 80 centimetre-long, heavy iron blade set on a metre-long wooden shaft was especially designed to bring down lions, and the 38 centimetre-long simi knives were double-bladed hand knives forged from melted-down car springs, and deadly. They were clearly not taking any chances. It was unusual for young men to accompany the herd boys on such an excursion. They might even have welcomed an attack, for killing a lion with a spear was a traditional rite of passage for local youths. Having despatched a lion, especially a magnificent male, a warrior would gain enviable status.

The lions, Mbili and Tatu in particular, stayed as quiet as they possibly could. One of the boys, though, was heading their way, beating the bushes with a stick. As he drew nearer, Mbili held his breath. He could have grabbed him and killed him in an instant, but it would have brought a terrible retribution on the pride. He remained motionless. The boy's stick was centimetres from Mbili's nose and, even though they were less than a metre apart, the boy did not see him. He walked on, still playing his game. The rest of the herdsmen and their cattle passed within 100 metres of the pride, and continued on to the river. When it seemed safe to do so, the lions left their cover and moved swiftly to another part of their territory.

For the pride, the drought was not a great hardship at first. As the herbivores became weaker from lack of food and water, they were easier to catch and, when they died, their bodies were scavenged. For the moment, however, life on the plains was almost in suspended animation – it was the 'great wait'.

Whether the lack of rain was due to climate change – a warming world – or to a natural cycle was unclear, but many of Nature's natural reservoirs, such as forests, had been damaged or destroyed, so the land had lost the ability to ride out the drought. Wildlife was as vulnerable to the change as the people, who, faced with famine, would be surviving on a thread. The months of poor rain were taking their toll.

The pride, however, was buffered against all this, at least in the short term. Mbili stood to welcome another hot, dry day. With the great buffalo herd firmly ensconced in their neighbours' territory, it was time for the pride to seek alternative prey. There were a few small surviving groups of wildebeest, zebra and gazelle but they were skittish and hard to approach. The lionesses were forced to look elsewhere, but the pickings were likely to be meagre.

Three of the junior lionesses were first to strike lucky when they intercepted an impala buck and contained their enthusiasm sufficiently to bring it down. However, along came Tatu, who immediately laid claim to the animal. The lionesses begrudgingly gave way, only to have the impala jump up and flee. Apart from a liberal coating of lion saliva, it was unhurt and bounded off into the bush, leaving five very embarrassed lions in its wake. Clearly, if the members of the pride were to survive they had to do better than that. Lions are less cooperative when hunting than one might imagine, and it was time to put the individual hunting skills to the test.

At dawn on the next day, the pride split into smaller groups. For their first time a bunch of youngsters left their home pride, at least temporarily, while the adult lionesses went foraging in twos and threes. Mbili and Tatu tagged along with Grandi, although Tatu had been sloping off on his own again lately, no doubt to a clandestine meeting with a neighbouring female.

The landscape, however, was almost bare. The drought was taking hold, the buffalo had moved on, and the animals on migration were far away. Until more thirsty and hungry animals started to succumb to the drought and the lions could either bring down the weak or scavenge their dead bodies, they could only hope for small fry. Grandi, along with Mbili and Tatu, was

walking across a small depression in the plain when she stopped
and began to dig. The two males nosed around inquisitively,
and they joined in the digging. Grandi had found the entrance
to a burrow and its occupant was at home. All three lions began
to dig, first using one forepaw and then the other, and
occasionally with both together. Mbili and Tatu quickly lost
interest and watched indifferently from nearby, but Grandi
continued to dig feverishly.

After about an hour, having excavated nearly three metres of
tunnel, she stopped and pushed her head down to take a look.
She jerked back quickly, and then ducked under once more.
Whatever was in the burrow was putting up a fight. She
grabbed it and started to pull, every muscle taut with the strain.
She released the prey momentarily and then seized it again,
finally hauling out, kicking and screaming, an adult female
warthog. A firm bite to the neck throttled the animal and
Grandi began to feed.

Seeing the food, Mbili and Tatu ambled across to take it
over, but Grandi was having none of it. She pushed back her
ears and hissed and snarled at the two males and they each took
a step back. A lioness with a small kill was usually left alone, and
Grandi was a stickler for tradition. Anyway, the warthog was
hardly worth the squabble, so the boys wandered a short way off
and lay down, hoping for bigger things. Grandi tucked in. She
had the entire beast to herself.

The youngsters were not so adept at catching their dinner.
They had cornered a warthog too, but a boar, and a smart one at
that. One of the young females spotted it first, at which time it was
unaware of the close proximity of the lions for it trotted through
some dried-up bushes without a care in the world. One of the
young male lions took off in a wide arc to intercept it, and another
young lioness came up behind it to complete the trap. The wily

warthog, however, stopped abruptly, raised its head and sniffed the air. They had been rumbled. Its extremely keen sense of smell picked up lion odour, so he ran for all he was worth out of harm's way. He moved so fast that the youngsters were unable to keep up, and one by one they dropped out of the chase.

The other group of young lions were equally inept, and one of their excursions ended in tragedy. They were stalking a full-size female rhino. She was quite emaciated but, as the young lions would find out, she still had plenty of fight in her. The lions surrounded her, and a young male, his mane no more than an untidy crew cut, began to dart in and out, trying to grab a leg. But every time he lunged forward she turned with extraordinary speed to face him. As a young lioness drew her defence, the male made another move, but he was not quick enough. The rhino turned and stabbed the lion several times with upward thrusts of its anterior horn. He fell to the ground, and the rhino gored him once in his neck and a second thrust went through his jaw and into his brain. He was killed instantly. The lionesses withdrew, and the rhino trotted away without further attacks. Vultures, followed closely by hyenas, quickly located the corpse. It was Kikuto. She took special pleasure in dissecting a lion, every mouthful a recompense for stricken clan mates. Within an hour there was very little of the young lion left, just a few fragments of flesh and a bloodstain on the ground. She cackled with satisfaction and led the clan away.

By April, the failure of the short rains during the previous November and December was having an even greater impact on wildlife. Water was scarce, and food for the large herbivores almost non-existent. In the south, the wildebeest had given birth to their calves but most were dying through lack of milk. Any that had survived were now buckling under the heat. Over a million wildebeest, 200,000 zebra and 300,000 Thomson's gazelles should have been preparing for their migration northwards and westwards, following the rains into the wooded areas. But there was no rain, and little prospect of it. The pastures in the migratory corridors were brown and dry. The animals were confused. They had nowhere to go.

The pride had reassembled so the lions were travelling around their territory more or less together. Tatu was gone for increasingly longer periods, but Mbili remained close to Grandi, ready to take advantage of her superior hunting skills. She was in the lead as usual and heading for the river. When they arrived, all they could see around them was devastation. They hesitated, as if taking in the horror of the scene before them. The river had largely dried up, just a few very shallow pools remaining, and mud that was once the riverbed was hard and cracked. The decomposing carcasses of several hippos were scattered about. They would have needed water and mud to cool and protect their huge bodies, but there was little left of either. Not far away and surrounded by clouds of flies, vultures and marabou storks were pecking at the withered corpse of a resident zebra. For the scavengers, it was an unexpected food bonanza, so the noble lions, including Mbili and Tatu, joined their ranks and tucked into the least putrefied of the hippo carcasses.

They had been with the dead hippos for more than an hour, when the lionesses from the neighbouring pride appeared on the other side of the dried riverbed. Grandi and the other lionesses were suddenly on full alert. Without the river barrier, they could simply walk straight into the Tingatinga Pride's territory. They stopped eating and snarled in the direction of the new arrivals. Tatu, though, seemed to be surprisingly well acquainted with them. He walked nonchalantly up to one of the leading lionesses. It was the female that had been with Tatu all those weeks ago and had been attacked by the Tingatinga lionesses. They rubbed heads and lay down. The lionesses followed suit. Mbili and the rest of his pride glared at them. Eventually Tatu rose, walked towards one of the hippos and resumed eating. The Makali Pride lionesses followed his example. So this clearly was where Tatu had been going – on a surreptitious but highly dangerous tryst with one of the Makali Pride females. He had been dicing with death, what with the three powerful males who protected their pride, but somehow he had come away unscathed.

So that was the way it was that day. Mbili and the Tingatinga Pride on one side of the riverbed, and Tatu with the Makali females on the other, both parties feasting on dead hippo, and both tolerating each other's presence – an uneasy truce . . . and there were plenty more hungry mouths arriving.

Hundreds more vultures dropped in to join the feast. They were Ruppell's griffon vultures, which had spent the night roosting on distant mountains to the south-east. During the hours of darkness, they were crowded on to ledges in vertical-sided gorges and, when the morning sun warmed the air, they spread their wide wings and rose on the thermals – rising columns of hot air – to great heights, from where they could spot the victims of the drought. They had soared almost effortlessly for over 150 kilometres to be at this dry riverbed and its rich supply of hippo meat. More usually they followed the great migration, but with the herds at a standstill and birthing over they were looking elsewhere for food. The early birds had spotted the carcasses from over three kilometres away and, as they dropped down, other birds watched their descent. Like a bush telegraph, birds were watching the behaviour of the birds ahead of them, until almost the entire colony was coming in to land, like aircraft arriving at a busy airport.

Among the early arrivals were other types of scavengers. First to spot the food had been white-headed vultures. They relied less on thermals to fly, so they were the first large birds airborne that morning. But even though they had sole access to the carcasses at first, they had to wait for the arrival of lappet-faced vultures, the strongest and most dominant birds. They bullied the other species but, with their powerful bills, they were able to slice through the tough skin, enabling not only themselves but also the other birds to get at the decomposing flesh.

With all this commotion in the air for all to see, it was inevitable that other scavengers were attracted too, and right on cue Kikuto and her clan of spotted hyenas appeared at the top of the embankment. On seeing the two lion prides, almost side-by-side, she was reluctant to approach any closer, but the smell of carrion was overpowering and much too inviting. She sauntered over to the nearest unoccupied carcass and began to feed. Mbili had already spotted her, but he was too busy taking what he could. Now, there were three deadly enemies eating within metres of each other, but all the usual rules of engagement had broken down. There was no time for fighting, only eating.

Time was called when the vultures flew en masse into the air. Grandi had had enough of eating with the enemy. She charged first at the hyenas, scattering them in every direction. Taking her cue, Mbili wrenched himself from his meat and joined the attack. Tatu, perhaps sensing that pride loyalty was at stake, ran over to Mbili, and the two of them pursued the hyenas across the plains. Kikuto escaped. Grandi then turned to the other pride. Snarling and hissing, she approached the rival lionesses aggressively. The other lionesses in her pride, together with the surviving youngsters, were right behind her.

Faced with the entire Tingatinga Pride, the intruders withdrew rapidly and returned to their side of the river. Reaching the top of the embankment, they paused momentarily and looked back, before disappearing over the rise and back into their own territory. There was still plenty, so the lionesses gorged themselves and then, as is the lion way, they took a drink at one of the remaining pools, and lay down and went to sleep.

By morning, Tatu had gone missing again, probably tempted away by those neighbouring lionesses. It is not uncommon for males of one pride to mate with unguarded females of another, and Tatu was doing just that. The difference this time was that he was going for longer. This made Mbili increasingly uneasy. He now had to protect the pride more or less on his own. Grandi and Old One Eye made up somewhat for Tatu's absence, roaring with Mbili in their lioness way and chasing hyenas, but should the migration arrive, then the number of nomadic lions sniffing around for poorly defended prides would increase. While drought hit the land, most animals were focussed entirely on basic survival, but if the rains came and the grass started to grow, then everything could change almost overnight. Already a rather odd couple had entered the pride's territory: an old male, way past his prime, and a young but aggressive lion ready to take on all-comers.

These two nomads strolled into the area, and the first the Tingatinga Pride knew about it was when several of its females were lazing around near a rocky outcrop. The older lion approached them first. He swaggered into view, head held high, and then he stood sideways on, his profile accentuating his supremacy, but they were not impressed. They charged without warning, and the old male lost all signs of dignity. He turned tail and fled. His younger companion, however, was less easily intimidated. He stood his ground, while the lionesses bared their teeth and snarled at him. He cuffed one of them and she stepped back. The others pushed forward but he simply glowered at them. They hissed, lunged and tried to slap the young lion's face with their claws.

Mbili heard the altercation. At first he walked but then trotted and finally charged. He slammed into the young pretender. The younger lion was taken aback, but tried to fight back. Mbili, though, had not lost his touch. The two lions were on their hind legs, cuffing and biting, but Mbili quickly wrestled his opponent to the ground, bit him hard on the rump so the blood flowed, and scratched his face so a deep wound appeared across his forehead and cheek. The intruder scrambled to his feet and ran, Mbili in hot pursuit. He chased him for over a kilometre before turning back to rejoin the lionesses. It was first blood to Mbili but, without Tatu around, he could hardly be expected to win every fight.

The lionesses had calmed down, and were laid down between the scattered rocks but, as Mbili walked past, one of them leapt to her feet, snarled at him and tried to slap him. He continued on his way without flinching. The pride females were especially tetchy at this time. New litters of cubs were on their way, the births timed to coincide with the glut of food that should arrive with the migration. Any intruders, especially nomadic males, would be a danger to their cubs' survival, so the lionesses were particularly aggressive towards other males and even other females, no matter who they were.

Some days later, the pride was close to its southern boundary, when Grandi spotted vultures circling in the distance. Mbili was apprehensive. Vultures usually meant a kill or a carcass, and a kill might be attended by powerful nomads or even the pride's southern neighbours, a smaller but still formidable group of lions with two mature males, one with a distinctive jet-black mane and a younger lion with a ginger mane. Without Tatu, Mbili could be compromised. Nevertheless, Grandi led the lionesses to investigate. They trotted at first, then slowed to a walk and stopped. Ahead of them, Kikuto and some of her hyena clan were whooping loudly while threatening a pair of lionesses. Between lunges at the hyenas, they were feeding on the carcass of a zebra that had succumbed to the drought. They were not from the neighbouring pride, but were nomads. When they saw the lionesses of the resident pride approaching, they backed off, moving to a short distance away, where they sat. The hyenas continued to circle, switching their harassment to the residents. Mbili, Grandi and others ignored them and quickly appropriated the food. They began to eat, but they were nervous.

Mbili leapt up, along with two of his lionesses, and they charged the nomads, chasing them to a patch of scrub roughly at the territorial boundary. Seizing the opportunity, Kikuto's hyenas dashed in to grab some meat. One ran away with a piece of leg in its jaws and another had the tail. Mbili raced back and the hyenas scattered, but he wasted no more time. He joined the lionesses at the carcass and they fed until they could feed no more.

A mighty roar from the other side of the scrub interrupted sleep. The neighbours were inspecting their boundary and testing for any signs of weakness next door. Mbili roared back, along with Grandi and some of the other lionesses, but the other pride was not fooled. The response from the Tingatinga Pride was a clear indication that only one male was present. The two pride males stared avidly into the Tingatinga Pride's territory. It would be an easy take-over, but they had to be sure. They would bide their time until the migration arrived, and the hunting was better, in more ways than one.

CHAPTER EIGHT

– Sinister Arrivals and Sudden Departures –

T he next dry season had started, and the arrival of the migration was still a month or two away . . . if it came at all. The long rains failed, the grass had not grown, and the great herds of wildebeest and zebra were still to appear. The failure brought famine. Even bodies to scavenge were few and far between, and the Tingatinga Pride was forced to hunt anything they could catch, no matter how small. The cubs had so far survived the disastrous weather but, having been introduced to the pride, they were having difficulty keeping up with the older lions as they meandered across their territory. Food was scarce, and the cubs were looking leggy and thin, and had little desire to play. They were at the end of the food queue, for milk was in short supply and they were often excluded at kills by the lionesses. If the kill was small, even their own mothers prevented them from feeding. Only Mbili allowed them to share his meal.

They trekked on, but when the pride reached its next stop, several of the older cubs were missing. They were seriously malnourished and had failed to keep up with pride so were left behind; such was the way of lions. There was prey nearby – gazelles and impala – but the cubs were far too young to hunt. They had to find the pride. It was the only way they could survive. They called in the vain hope they might make contact with the others.

Some distance away the lionesses called too. It was a beacon by which their lost youngsters might find them again. Even one of the juvenile males, suffering from malnourishment but still able to keep up with the pride, joined the despondent chorus for his sisters and brothers. But the cubs were just too far away. There were no replies. After an hour of calling, the lionesses moved on, their surviving cubs just about keeping up. They had to move to a remote part of their territory if they were to find prey.

Eventually, they were forced to rest in the shade of a tree. And as they lay there, the forlorn figure of one of the cubs appeared on a rise. She called, the pride responded and, ever so slowly, she limped into camp. Somehow, she had found the energy to keep going. She was very weak and had not eaten for several days, but if she could stick with the pride now, she had a chance. She flopped on to the ground next to her mother. She received a barrage of licks, and was fast asleep within minutes.

Meanwhile, Grandi had seen a warthog in the open and began to stalk it, while Old One Eye ran to outflank it from the cover of some bushes and trees. The temperature was soaring and the air shimmered, but the two cats had only one thing on their mind. The warthog continued to snuffle about on the ground, rooting for tubers and bulbs, but its sixth sense made it look up. At that moment, Grandi started her run. The prey took off at high speed, but she had no need to waste too much energy. Within seconds, Old One Eye had run in from the side and grabbed the boar by the scruff of the neck. It screamed, but as soon as Grandi arrived, she grabbed its throat and suffocated it. The rest of the pride piled in. It was a most welcome meal, but each of the pride had barely a few bites.

All around them dust swirled across the plains, the scorching wind gathering up shrivelled plants and carrying them to who knows where. An ostrich, its legs invisible in the shimmering heat haze, seemed to float rather walk across the plain. The landscape was tinder dry, but many creatures could get by with whatever they found scattered on the ground. Guinea fowl scratched at the parched ground, sending up tiny clouds of dust wherever they trod. Savannah mice were thriving because of a superabundance of seeds amongst the dried grass stems; and wherever there are small rodents there are sure to be smaller predators around ready to catch them. And, sure enough, an African wild cat was out and about catching mice and feeding its kitten. Unlike the lion cubs, the wild cat kitten was positively thriving. It would not go hungry.

Even bigger animals were buffered from the drought by the food that they ate. A herd of kudu chewed on the flame-red flowers in combretum thickets, which bloomed even in the drought. Giraffes and impala were feasting on acacia leaves, and so kept in good condition, even during this driest of droughts for many years. They acquired most of the nutrients and water they needed from the leaves themselves, but shortly even those would be gone. There was one more force of nature with which to contend – fire.

Mbili was the first to wrinkle his nose. It was a familiar smell, and it stank of danger. He rose and looked out over the plain. A short distance away a wall of orange flames leaped into the sky and a plume of black smoke hung menacingly overhead. The smell of burned wood and straw filled the air. Herdsmen outside the Tingatinga Pride's territory had started fires to clear land, but the fires had got out of hand and they were moving unbelievably fast to where the pride was holed up. In a very short time the plains all around them were ablaze. They were trapped.

The lionesses gathered up the cubs and ran to where the fire seemed less intense, but they were beaten back by the heat. They fled in the opposite direction only to be stopped by another firestorm. The smoke was becoming thick and choking, but by keeping low the lionesses and their cubs were able to breathe. Then, Grandi noticed a possible escape route. Two large boulders on some rocky land prevented the fire from reaching the ground, but all around there were flames. It was a tunnel of living flames, and it was their only way out. Grandi went first, then Ndugu with the young cubs. Old One Eye led the rest of the lionesses and the older cubs, and Mbili brought up the rear.

For the few moments they were in the tunnel it was terrifying, but they all made it through. Mbili's mane was singed but otherwise he came out unscathed. On the other side they all could breathe once more, and they ran as fast as they could to stay ahead of the advancing wildfires. All around them, hawks and other birds flew towards the flames rather than away from them. They swooped down to catch the insects and other creatures that were escaping from the flames. Even in the face of total destruction there were animals that profited from the misfortune of others. But there was another new development. It was not only the grass that was burning, but also any cover that remained. Surviving the fire was one thing, but losing the cover was another. Prey animals could no longer hide from their predators and the predators could no longer hide from their prey. It was a disaster.

Eventually, the fires burned themselves out, but even while the vegetation was still smouldering, some animals returned. Small herds of impala walked amongst the debris, searching out any greenery that survived. They did not have the benefit of cover, but they still had the speed and agility to outrun predators, but for some of their relatives the sudden absence of bushes and thickets put them at a distinct disadvantage, and Grandi was quick to take advantage of it.

The steenbok depends on cover to survive. Its predator avoidance strategy is simply to remain still amongst the bushes. With its chestnut-coloured coat it would normally be well hidden, but now it was not. It might have thought it was safe, sitting on the ground with its legs tucked under its body, but it was there for all to see.

Grandi stalked right up to it in the open, from directly behind, so it could not see her approach. She started her run and still the animal did not move. At the last moment, it leaped to its feet and started to flee, but it was too late. It tried its more usual tactic of changing direction abruptly but Grandi put out her forepaw and tripped it up. It tumbled, scrambled to its feet, but another cuff slammed it back on to the ground. She bit into the neck, held tight and the animal was dead. It was not the biggest of antelopes, no more than a few mouthfuls for the assembled lions, but it was well-needed food. The pride gathered around and ate the lot.

It was not that long after the fires had died down that Tatu returned from another of his long absences and, after an especially long trek, the entire pride entered rocky thorn bush country that had been untouched by the wildfires. It was in the north of their range, but it was hot. Biting tsetse flies were common and they had to watch out for local herdsmen. For the moment, they lay down beneath a tall African ebony tree or jackalberry, named for the jackal's fondness for its fruits. It was not jackals, however, that broke the peace but a troop of baboons. They had been resting in the tree before the lions arrived, but now they were trapped. They could not get down to forage because every time one of them tried a lioness would chase it back up again. They were getting impatient, but all they could do was wait until the lions finally went to sleep. Then, first one and then another lowered themselves gently to the ground, followed by the entire troop. As they disappeared over a rise one of the lionesses awoke, raised her head and stood up. She strolled quietly to the small hill and sat down, eagerly watching what the baboons would do next.

At first, the troop fanned out and foraged on the ground, plucking seed heads and pulling up dried shoots, but then she noticed one of the large and powerful male baboons behaving in an odd way. He was picking up pieces of vegetation, but did not appear to be eating. He was trying, almost desperately, to be indifferent to the presence of a gazelle mother and her fawn not far away. Somehow, the gazelles here were not only surviving the drought but had also given birth. The baboon shuffled about – a poor actor – but he was edging gradually closer to two gazelles, while not causing them to bolt. The gazelle, though, spotted his strange behaviour, so mother and fawn trotted away to a safer distance. At this, the baboon simply targeted another gazelle mother and went through his excruciating performance all over again.

This time, the mother was not so alert. When the baboon was just a few metres from the pair, it suddenly charged. The mother leapt into the air, but the fawn was not so quick. With a lightning grab, the baboon caught it and bit into its neck, it was dead instantly. At this, the lioness raced down the slope towards the baboon, but it saw the cat coming, dropped the fawn and ran for its life. The lioness ignored the baboon, took the fawn, and started to eat. She had had no more than a mouthful when a hyena turned up. It stopped a few metres from the lioness, sat down and stared at the dead fawn. The lioness looked up as several more arrived. It was not Kikuto's clan. They were unusually silent and quite unnerving. After five or ten minutes there were 20 of them, either lying or sitting, all looking intently at the lioness and her meal. She put her head down to take another bite and suddenly one started to whoop. It was the signal for the attack. The hyenas surrounded the lioness and were closing the circle. One after the other, they lunged at her. She dropped the food and ran back over the rise.

A few minutes later, the cavalry arrived. Mbili, together with Tatu, Grandi and two lionesses came running over the hill and charged down on to the hyenas. They fled for their lives, two individuals carrying between them what remained of the dead fawn. They were chased for less than a kilometre, at which point Mbili and the others gave up and returned to the pride. It was early evening, and time to hunt, if only they could find something to kill. They hid in an area of long grass and waited for something to walk by.

Their first chance came when another herd of Thomson's gazelle came close, but the buck picked up the lions' scent and the entire group bolted. Grandi, however, was as quick as lightning and cuffed the hind legs of a fleeing doe and brought it down. Within an hour, the gazelle was consumed, and the area must have reeked of lion and blood, yet a second group entered the same area. The lions let several animals pass before they attacked, and despite rushing the animals when they were only a few metres away, they all escaped in the confusion. And then, against all the odds, the same group retraced it steps and was attacked yet again. This time Grandi set up her attack so that she aimed ahead of the moving target. Instead of rushing the gazelles haphazardly, she targeted two – a doe and fawn. She stalked them carefully, staying low for as long as she could. Meanwhile, two of the other lionesses about ten metres apart lay down ahead of the herd, but one of them shifted her position and was spotted. The gazelles bolted, one leaping almost into Grandi. She lunged, the gazelle jinked, and it was gone.

By this time, one of the smaller hunting units was a kilometre downstream beside the dried riverbed where some of the gazelles had regrouped. By now they were so nervous, almost anything would have spooked them. A doe and a buck were a few metres away from the rest. Suppressing the instinctive urge to chase after them, one of the young lionesses walked slowly, almost casually, towards them. She was becoming increasingly more skilled at hunting, and had teamed up temporarily with Old One Eye. The one-eyed lioness kept back, watching what her companion was doing. When the youngster had reached the critical flight distance, the gazelles looked up and then started to run. The younger lioness ran to one side of them, and the buck inexplicably doubled back right into the path of Old One Eye. She leapt, slamming into the side of the poor creature and they both rolled in a cloud of dust, stopped only by a dried-up bush. A bite to throat was held for a few minutes and the gazelle was dead.

Tatu had been watching from the sidelines. He walked arrogantly from a thicket in which he had been hiding and headed towards the two lionesses with their kill. This time, Old One Eye was not going to give in so easily. She snarled at Tatu, bared her teeth, and leaped at him. Taken aback, he stopped, paused and then attacked her viciously. He grabbed her, shook her old body violently and broke her back in two places. The younger cat ran back to find the pride, while Tatu settled down to feed, the ill-fated lioness lying dead by his side. It was not the first time that Tatu had been surprisingly aggressive towards his own pride mates, and it would not be the last. Any natural order that there was in the pride seemed to be breaking down.

By now, the second litter of youngsters were almost adult and becoming a liability, especially with the shortage of easy-to-catch food. The older members of the pride, as well as the perpetually aggressive Tatu, were beginning to show signs of irritation. Even Mbili had been short-tempered with the young males of late, and Grandi had been equally aggressive towards the young females. It would not be long before they were forced to leave the pride. The youngsters had learned well from the lionesses, so they would be well prepared to fend for themselves, as long as the drought would break.

The young males were first to be sent away, chased across the plain by Mbili and Tatu for several kilometres. There was no remorse, no heartache, no sadness – none of those human emotions at parting with a loved one. The young females and the underdeveloped Ndugu, though, tried to stay with the pride for a while longer. Ndugu's mane was much scraggier than those of his male siblings and, all told, he was less well developed. He was gangly, awkward, shy and less likely to join in pride activities. He simply watched and waited for the food to arrive, but he was always last to feed, even after the new cubs. Even though he should have been gone, he followed the pride and when the other lions rested, he would lay some forty or so metres away. The older lionesses had the habit of chasing him but he always came back, sometimes accepted temporarily as one of the group and other times forced to live on the periphery. He was attacked several times, particularly when he came close to the new cubs but, as the cubs grew and any threat he might pose diminished, he was acknowledged gradually as one of the pride once more, and he began to reprise his old role as guardian of the nursery. Outside, he would have been killed within days, but with his pride mates Ndugu was relatively safe.

The young females were not so lucky. Despite their usefulness during hunts, their time was coming too. They increasingly found themselves ostracised by the other members. They would lay some distance from the main group. Sometimes, one of the older females would walk over to the youngsters and rub heads briefly, but the behaviour was perfunctory. The problem was they appeared less confident, and to be an accepted member of the pride an individual must be self-assured. On one occasion, following a brief head-rubbing session, the youngsters got up, but instead of walking away with assurance, one of them turned her head back to look at the pride. She was immediately attacked and chased. Eventually, several of the young females were chased away too. This meant the pride had shrunk somewhat, fewer mouths to feed; and there was one more absent again – Tatu.

Dark thunderclouds appeared over distant mountains. The air was still, humidity rising – a change in the weather. A flicker of far-off lightning and a deep rumble announced the start of the rains and an end to the drought. Gradually more clouds scudded across the vast open skies, closing out the blue and replacing it with grey.

Great pillars of rain separated by shafts of sunlight united the sky with the ground. They drifted across the plains like floating giants, saturating everything in their paths. During the drought, the lions had been surprisingly well fed. They had scavenged carcasses, staked out waterholes and harassed thirsty and hungry buffalo, but when the rains came, the large plant-eaters on which lions depended – antelope, zebra, gazelles and buffalo – became more scattered. Generally, lions let the prey come to them, but now they had to go to the prey . . . if they could find it. And the arrival of the rains would have a surprising outcome. For the Tingatinga lions, they brought famine, not food.

The morning sky was like golden porridge. A line of tiny wildebeest silhouettes streamed past a lone, flat-topped acacia tree on the horizon. The land was still as black as night, but when the top of the sun appeared, it caused a wispy mist to form just above the ground. The rains had come and the grass had grown again. It was going to be a brilliant day and, as the light brightened, it became clear a miracle had occurred. As far as the eye could see there were wildebeest, hundreds of thousands of them. The sound of their recognizable and relentless grunting and snorting filled the air. The empty plains had filled overnight with a superabundance of life. The migration had arrived at last . . . but it was on the other side of the river, in Makali Pride country.

The Tingatinga Pride had returned to their eastern boundary, on the west bank of the main river. The great herds of wildebeest were tantalisingly close. Animals would come down to drink, the best time to catch them unawares, but they were firmly in the neighbour's territory and they were reaping the benefits. Time and again, the rumble of hooves and clouds of dust were sure signs that they were hunting very successfully, but the Tingatinga Pride was still feeding on small fry.

Tatu was away as usual, probably somewhere on the other side of the river, chasing the neighbouring females, but Mbili and the lionesses were reluctant to cross. Their rivals still had three powerful males, and with Mbili defending the group alone, they would be highly vulnerable to a takeover. However, hunger eventually got the better of them, and one evening they waded across the river. The river was relatively high, so they were up to their necks in water. Nevertheless, they all made it to the other side without drowning or being caught by crocodiles, and they quickly hid in a patch of long grass for animals to come down to the water to drink. They let several animals pass them by, but Grandi had already spotted one with a slight limp, no doubt an injury sustained during a stampede while escaping the Makali Pride. She waited until it lowered its head to drink and then charged out of the grass at breakneck speed. The kill was easy. She leaped on to the animal, brought it down and grabbed its throat. The rest of the pride, including Mbili, piled in. After a few slaps, snarls and general pushing and shoving, the cats tucked in. They ate nervously, looking up every few minutes in case the neighbours should appear, but their activity was no longer a secret. Vultures circled and began to drop down, and this brought Kikuto and her hyenas from their wallow in the marsh. Soon, there was pandemonium. The pride made a tactical retreat. They quickly crossed the river without incident and climbed the bank. They stopped as they reached the top of the embankment and looked back. Their exit was timely. The three Makali Pride males walked cautiously into the clearing and towards the remains of the wildebeest. They sniffed the ground and scent marked around the carcass, and finally took possession. They knew their neighbours had been there. They could smell them. Two of the lions roared, but there was no reply. Mbili and the rest of the Tingatinga Pride slunk away. No return roars, no noise – they just melted into the bush and were gone.

The next morning, after an unsuccessful night's hunting, the pride returned to the river but, as they came to the top of the embankment, they were brought up short. Down by the water's edge were the Makali Pride males and several of their lionesses, and they were on the Tingatinga Pride's side of the river. One of the lions looked up and spotted Mbili. The intruder roared but did not wait for a reply. He and the other males gave chase. Mbili turned and ran. The intruders kept roaring as they were running, and one caught up briefly, cuffing Mbili on the rear leg. It was the spur he needed and he put on a sudden spurt of speed, leaving his pursuers behind; but he ran and ran until he disappeared over the next hill.

Two of the Tingatinga Pride lionesses, meanwhile, gathered up their cubs and ushered them to safety in the thick vegetation of the nearby marsh. The other lionesses set up a diversion. They burst from the long grass, Grandi in the lead, and chased the intruding females back across the river. The males, having seen off Mbili, doubled back and went in search of the cubs. All three of them headed for the marsh, but one of the lionesses guarding the cubs ran out and drew them away. Grandi and the others came back to harass the males, their more slender and agile bodies enabling them to stay out of harm's way, but then they were backed into an area of long grass. The males did not follow but flopped down on the ground and waited.

No one moved. The neighbouring lionesses were back on their side of the river, the Tingatinga cubs and one female were in the marsh, Grandi and the other lionesses were in the long grass, Mbili was about a kilometre away firmly humiliated, and the intruders were out in the open; and that was the way it was for the rest of the day. By evening, the males had had enough and re-crossed the river, while their females set out for a night's hunting.

The Tingatinga females and their cubs were reunited. None of them was hurt. Mbili walked back cautiously, fearing the worst, but a head-rubbing session with Grandi and a couple of the other lionesses reassured him that things were all right. They moved away from their eastern boundary, and into the centre of their home range. The neighbours had tested the Tingatinga Pride's defences and had found them wanting. They would be back; you could be sure of that.

But it was not the Makali Pride that was to make the first serious incursion. The two males from the neighbouring pride in the south were testing the waters too. They moved gingerly into their neighbour's territory, and were on full alert when they came across four of the Tingatinga females. The lionesses were walking in single file down a track, heading towards a small stream, when they saw a small herd of gazelle drinking. One lioness continued to move forward while the others stopped and waited. The two males stopped too, and watched from the cover of an acacia thicket. The gazelles spotted the lioness advancing towards them and trotted quietly away, but when she broke into a gallop, two of them doubled back and ran straight into the other three lionesses. They rushed them and brought down a young buck.

This was the cue for the two males to make their appearance. It was not unusual for males of one pride to take an interest in the females of another, just as Tatu had been doing. Hot-blooded males were always on the lookout for mating opportunities. In their own pride, all their cubs were about a year old, which meant they followed their mothers wherever they went. They were no longer at risk of being killed by nomadic or neighbouring males. So the black-maned males could afford to spend time away from their pride, and foster a relationship with neighbouring females.

They walked casually towards the four females, sniffing the ground as they went. One was older and bolder than the other, but both were full-grown and at their peak in condition. Their manes blew in the wind, and they strutted the final few metres with their heads held high. The lionesses were not concerned for their own safety, however, for the amorous behaviour of these two beaux was a welcome distraction from their daily routine, but they *were* anxious for their cubs that were hidden not far away. If these two picked up their scent, they could kill all of them.

As a precaution, one of the lionesses left their kill and charged straight at the older of the two males. She carried her head low, her ears set back and she snarled and hissed with her mouth open and her large canine teeth clearly visible. The lion stopped, stood erect and was about to attack, when a second lioness charged him. The two intruders fled with the two lionesses in pursuit. The females gave up the chase after a few metres and simply stared at the two males as they reached the top of a rise and looked back. Mbili was on a hilltop behind them. He roared at the two intruders, but was careful to keep a respectful distance. He could not take them on alone, but no doubt hoped that his token defiance was enough to keep them at bay for a little while longer.

When Tatu was absent it was up to the females of the pride to help defend the cubs. Hyenas were a constant danger, but the imminent threat was from these other pride males and nomads intent on taking over their pride. Sensing the weakness in having only one male around, the males from the south made several forays into their neighbours' territory. It came to a head when they began deliberately and systematically to hunt down the cubs.

Mbili roared at the intruders, but he was chased for his trouble and nearly caught. Fortunately, Ndugu had hidden them well in the marsh, and lay nearby, guarding them as best as he could.

The invaders let Mbili be and turned their attention to the marsh. They could smell Ndugu, but could not see him, and they knew better than to enter the marsh with a defensive lion on the loose; but then they picked up the scent of the cubs. They curled their lips and grimaced, and then prowled back and forth beside the thick vegetation. There was no doubt that these two would kill all the cubs if they could get at them. Ndugu was understandably anxious. He dared not move or make a sound, but he somehow had to summon help.

Grandi and the other lionesses were a short distance away but unaware that Mbili had been chased and that the cubs were in danger. They ambled across the plain, looking out for anything that might constitute food. It was then that they heard a roar, Ndugu's roar. He had taken a chance. Grandi immediately started to run towards the sound; the other females following close behind. When they saw the neighbours, they hesitated, then inched forward slowly, a pace at a time. Their hair bristled, and they hissed and snarled. The males did not budge. They were not so easily intimidated. They brought themselves up to their full height and, with heads held high, they strutted towards Grandi, clearly the leader. She, in turn, did not waver. The males halted. They were unused to such boldness. The other lionesses held back, several paces behind Grandi, and the lioness in the marsh remained hidden. The cubs cowered in a depression, surrounded by reeds. For the moment, it was stalemate.

The older of the males twitched, and then moved. Grandi snarled, but he was only going to lie down. The younger lion followed his example, and one by one the lionesses sat down too; all, that is, except Grandi. She remained standing, ready for any tricks the two males might play. The silence was broken by the call of a small bird – a rufous-naped lark – perched on a thorn bush. Each little rendition of *tseep-tseeoo* was interspersed with fluttering leaps and the raising of his crest, but the lions ignored the recital and stared at the ground instead.

The stand-off lasted for more than an hour, by which time Grandi had also relented. She sat on her haunches, but with every nerve and muscle ready to react. The two males seemed extraordinarily relaxed, so when they got slowly to their feet, the lionesses stayed put; all except Grandi. They sauntered towards the marsh area where Ndugu and the cubs were hiding, but Grandi leaped up and ran quickly to put herself between the marsh and the two males. Instantly, the other lionesses rose. The older male snarled and rushed forward, catching Grandi with a powerful blow to the face. She was knocked off her feet and went rolling in the dust. The others drew back. At that moment, Mbili appeared. He had doubled back and had been watching the group for some time, unsure of what to do next, but the moment he saw Grandi fall he raced down the slope and made straight for her attacker. Taken by surprise, the black-maned male took the full force of Mbili's charge. The two went tumbling to the ground in clouds of red dust. Instantly, both were on their feet and clawing and biting at each other's head and neck. The fury with which they fought was unbelievable. The lionesses just stood and stared.

Animals all around stopped what they were doing and turned their heads to listen to the guttural roars and growls. Mbili seemed to dominate the fight, so the younger male stood back, watched and waited, ready to run if necessary. But the older male's claw became caught in Mbili's mane, so Mbili had his weight pulling down on his neck. This gave him a disadvantage, and so the fight shifted the other way, the black-maned male raining blow upon blow to the side of Mbili's face with the right forepaw while desperately trying to extricate his left paw. The younger lion sensed this was his opportunity to join in, and he lunged at Mbili's rump and took a bite. The bite made him lurch to one side, freeing up the black-maned male. Now Mbili was fighting not one but two strong males, and he was taking a pounding. Blood poured from deep gashes in his face and side and, after 30 minutes of continuous fighting, he was beginning to weaken.

Then another miracle happened. Tatu appeared. He tore into the two intruders like an animal possessed. Mbili got his second wind, and the two brothers fought side-by-side like demons. The younger, ginger-maned male was first to give up. He turned and ran, closely followed by the black-maned male. Mbili and Tatu chased them for several kilometres, until they had cleared the brothers' territory. They would not be back in a hurry.

The lionesses gathered around their two conquerors. They rubbed heads, licked wounds and generally made a fuss of the two brothers; then they all flopped down to rest. It had been quite a day.

With Tatu back in the pride, life became relatively quiet. Nomads – coalitions of males and groups of related females – were arriving with the migration, but so far none dared challenge the two brothers. The migration itself had remained on the far side of the river, so food was still scarce in the Tingatinga Pride's territory. One female brought down a warthog, and in the ensuing brawl several of her pride mates slapped and spat until the carcass was subject to a tug of war in which none of them would let go of the pig. Eventually, the warthog was rent asunder, each lioness retiring with her own small portion.

The pride's luck changed, however, when a young elephant stumbled into view. It must have become separated from the rest of its herd, or poachers had killed its mother. It was no more than a metre-and-a-half tall, but it was still a strong and formidable opponent. The lionesses surrounded it, while keeping well clear at first. The elephant trumpeted and swung its head from side to side. It may have been a youngster but it was armed with a pair of tusks, which could cause severe injuries if they skewered a lion. The lionesses goading the elephant from the front kept well clear, while Grandi and Umbu tackled the rear.

It was Grandi who made the first attack. She grabbed the back of the elephant's rear leg and bit hard, severing the main tendons. Now the beast was unable to walk properly, and so Umbu seized the opportunity to come up under its chin and grab it by the underside of the neck. The bite to the throat restricted the elephant's windpipe and it slowly succumbed, eventually toppling over. It died just as Mbili and Tatu arrived to take over the carcass, but there was plenty for all the pride so when the two boys were sated the lionesses piled in. Chica went to fetch the cubs, and so they all ate well that night, and for the next couple of days.

It was about this time that Chipipi, the youngest of the adult lionesses, was due to give birth. She was out of sync with the other females, so not only would she have to raise her cubs alone initially, but she would also not be able to follow the pride for several weeks. And if that was not enough, she was not a particularly good mother anyway.

One night, when the rest of the pride was some distance away, she hid her two cubs and went out in search of food. She struck lucky, chancing upon a zebra that had died of old age. She fed on the carcass and then went to fetch her offspring.

While she was gone a male leopard discovered the remains and ate what it could before the mother returned. As she approached, it shinned up a nearby tree, so the mother had a predicament. She could only bring one cub at a time, so she would have had to leave one cub by the carcass, while she fetched the second. But she knew the leopard was there, so every time she was about to go for another cub, she would hesitate and return immediately to the first one. Then confusion got the better of her and she went to fetch the second cub. The leopard clambered down the tree, grabbed the first cub, biting it deeply in the chest. It died instantly. When the mother returned empty-handed, the leopard dropped the cub and scrambled back up the tree. The lioness went straight for the dead cub, sniffed it, licked it and, as it did not move, she went back in search of her other cub.

The leopard, meanwhile, dropped down again, ignored the dead cub and feasted on the zebra. The lioness was over a kilometre away and failed to find her other cub for some time. She grunted loudly, and waited for a reply. The cub bleated quietly and, after a 15-minute search in the dark, eventually she found it. She picked it by the scruff of the neck and carried it to the zebra carcass, stopping from time to time to re-adjust her grip.

As they approached, the leopard climbed back up the tree and embarked on what turned out to be a very long wait. He had to remain patiently in the tree for most of the night, because the mother continued to feed, and then went to sleep by the carcass, seemingly oblivious to the dead cub beside her and the leopard in the tree above her.

At first light, the leopard tried to make its escape, but just as it reached the ground, Mbili and Tatu arrived. He tried to scramble back up but one cuff from Mbili's front paw brought him tumbling back down. Tatu immediately set about him, biting and clawing the unfortunate beast. Defence was useless under the onslaught of these two powerful lions. His neck was bitten, his backbone broken and his belly slit open. As Mbili, Tatu and the mother and cub walked away, the vultures gathered to clean up the mess; but the tragedy was not over yet. When the small group of lions sat down to rest, Tatu rolled accidentally on the surviving cub and squashed it. None of the young mother's cubs survived.

In fact, the pride seemed to be lurching from one disaster to the next, with another following soon after Chipipi's tragedy. Spurred on by their previous success at bringing down an elephant, the lionesses tried again. This time they surrounded an elephant calf that had been playing in a pool while its mother was feeding nearby. They taunted the baby, in an attempt to make it leave the wallow, but it ignored the lions and continued to splash about in the mud. Losing patience, Grandi leapt on to the elephant's back and tried to topple it over. At this, the baby trumpeted loudly and its mother came running, along with the rest of the herd. Grandi leaped to the ground and the lions scattered, but the elephants were not leaving it at that. They smelled the air, trampled the vegetation, and searched hard and long. It was clear they were looking for the lion cubs.

Ndugu quickly rounded them up and ushered them first to the long grass, then an acacia thicket and finally towards a rocky gorge, where they could take refuge in small caves on the steep slopes. The elephants followed. First they went to the long grass and flattened it. Anything hiding there would not have survived. Then they followed the scent to the acacia thicket and tore the bushes apart. They were working systematically along the route the cubs had taken, and they were catching up fast. Ndugu tried to get the last of the cubs into a cave, but it was too late. The lead elephant – the matriarch – brushed Ndugu aside with one sweep of her trunk and caught one of the cubs. She held it high in the air and, with a loud trumpeting, dashed it to the ground. It died instantly. The mother of the calf that had been attacked, her calf in tow, came and trampled the corpse and, having taken revenge, the herd quietly and orderly walked away.

Only a few of the pride's current litter had survived, but even then these were not safe from the vagaries of the savannah. When food was in short supply, they were abandoned deliberately. At other times they were abandoned by accident, and such a calamity occurred when the pride visited a waterhole in the west of the home range. Ndugu was on nursery duty as usual and the pride with all its surviving cubs gathered at the water's edge to drink. When Grandi finished, the others finished too, and she led them away in single file along the floor of a deep ravine. Ndugu and the cubs brought up the rear; all, that is, except one little fellow. He was playing about with the water and failed to see that others were leaving. By the time they were half-a-kilometre away, he realised he was alone, and rushed up and down bleating and miaowing loudly. His cries went unheard. They carried on the wind, but it was blowing in the wrong direction. Kikuto and a couple of her cohorts appeared, as if on cue. It meant that there was one cub less.

The pride seemed blissfully unaware that the number of cubs was dwindling, for they had more pressing needs. Unlike neighbouring prides, which were enjoying wildebeest and zebra aplenty, the Tingatinga pride was still on emergency rations. The migration had not reached them, and they dared not enter the Makali Pride territory on the other side of the main river lest they be attacked by the bigger pride. They continued to criss-cross their own territory in search of anything vaguely edible.

It was on one such trek that they found an old bull buffalo in a wallow. The weight of years was pressing down on his tired body so he had not bothered to keep up with his herd, and was living a solitary bachelor life. Claw marks down the side of his body and a shredded ear were signs that he had had a run in with lions quite recently, but he had clearly fought them off and survived. There was plenty of fight yet in the old boy, so he would be a tough opponent. However, the Tingatinga Pride had become quite adept at taking out these powerful beasts during the drought, so there was no hesitation in having a go at this one, but first they had to wait for him to emerge from the mud. The lions settled down a short distance away and slept.

The buffalo finished his ablutions and emerged from the wallow caked in a generous layer of mud. He walked slowly and deliberately, his bones pushing up visibly beneath a thick hide that was hanging loose from the crest of his spine. His horns looked enormous, but they were battered and chipped and seemed to weigh heavy on his old, broad head. He was heading towards the long grass and the promise of an evening meal. As he walked and chomped he resembled a grass mower slowly cutting a lawn. The pride, however, were still asleep and so had not noticed he was gone.

The alarm call of a baboon brought the pride to its feet. The troop was in a nearby greenheart tree, plucking fruit. Some were up in the branches causing the plum-like fruits to fall, while others gathered them up below. One of the tree climbers had spotted the lions, and gave a bark. The rest stopped what they were doing and clambered up to join him. They were safe as long as they stayed in the tree. Grandi walked over to the tree, reached up and raked her claws down its trunk. A young female leaped up, to the consternation of the baboons that chattered and barked noisily, and slowly slithered down again. There was much head rubbing and yawning, and the surviving cubs chased and played with a scattering of white bones from an old leopard kill.

Grandi looked down to the mud wallow and saw that the old buffalo had moved on. She looked around, searching for any signs of him, and then she spotted some movement in the long grass. That was him. She led the way, the rest of the pride following behind her. Mbili and Tatu remained at the rest site, along with Ndugu and the cubs, which meant the troop of baboons was forced to remain in the tree. They quietened down and made the most of the feeding opportunity; after all, they could not get down.

The lions entered the long grass, but they were upwind of the buffalo. He raised his head and his broad nostrils took in the air and the odour of lions. He seemed unconcerned; after all, he was a bull buffalo and nobody tangles with his kind. He went on munching the grass. The lions waited. They would be at a disadvantage if caught up in the long grass, so they would bide their time until he emerged. They left and flopped down in a thicket, and then did what lions do best – they slept again.

By sunset, the buffalo had finished and was heading back to the wallow, but this brought him on a collision course with the pride. By the time he brushed past the thicket it was too late. The lionesses leaped up and were harassing him, but this buffalo was a wily old beast. He simply backed up against a tree so that none of them could get behind him and swung his mighty head from side to side. The lions dare not go too close, but tried to manoeuvre him from his refuge while keeping clear of his menacing horns. He grunted and they snarled, but he would not budge.

After an hour of taunting, the lionesses seemed to lose interest. They yawned and then sat or laid down a few metres from the bull. He continued to stand, almost motionless, just the gentle swaying of his head as he scanned his surroundings. Then, he too succumbed to fatigue and began to lie down. It was what they had been waiting for. The cats jumped up immediately, ready to attack, forcing the buffalo to stand again if he was not to be overwhelmed. Again, it was deadlock. The cats stared at the buffalo and the buffalo stared back, saliva dribbling down his slack jaws. He shuffled forwards a little, and Umbu was able to slip around behind the tree unseen. It was just enough for her to leap on to his back. In a sudden release of pent-up energy, the bull bucked and kicked, and swung his horns. At the same time, another lioness sank her claws into the thick skin of his rump and Grandi tried to go for his throat, but they both had to leap away as his horns swept down towards them. The jockey, though, slipped and came tumbling off the buffalo's back. He turned, hooked her with his horn and, with a deft upward flick, ripped into her abdomen and then trampled her head. She died instantly. Grandi and the other cats jumped back, but he was away from the tree. Now they could bring him down with the sheer weight of numbers. He snorted through flared nostrils, and the whites of his eyes showed the fear and loathing he had for these terrifying predators. It would not be long. In minutes, they would choke the life out of him, but first they had to topple him.

After another 15 minutes of lunges and counter-lunges, the buffalo staggered and fell on his side. One of the lionesses grabbed his thigh and tried to turn him on his back, but the beast raised his head momentarily and then lay still again. The other lionesses did not move, the brief rest sufficient to enable him to get up again. The same lioness grabbed his shoulder and tried to pull him back down, but he whirled around and missed goring her by centimetres. With the buffalo in pursuit, she ran to a fallen tree and clambered into its branches so she was clear of the ground. Away from his refuge the buffalo was now more vulnerable, but the agility of this large and tired animal was awesome. As two of the lionesses tried to attack from behind, he swirled around and faced them. There were claw marks all over his hide, a deep cut across his face, his tail had been bitten badly, and his old, aching body seemed to be at the point of giving up, yet still he fought back. For another hour, he charged the cats, while they leaped at him, but they could not bring him down again.

Suddenly, Grandi stopped her attack. She looked up into the sky. In the twilight, she could see great swirls of dust heading their way. It was the migration and it was crossing the river. One by one the lionesses broke away. With Grandi in the lead, they trotted away, leaving the old buffalo standing alone and confused. There were easier pickings heading their way. It was time to hunt wildebeest again. The buffalo headed off in the opposite direction and walked, rather unsteadily at first, towards the wallow, where he would immerse himself in the rejuvenating mud. He had been saved by the migration.

Grandi headed for the river. Even Mbili and Tatu were moved to follow. A few heavy showers had fallen on their side of their border, a magnet for the wildebeest herds. As usual, they poured into the river where many were drowned accidentally or grabbed by crocodiles. They clambered up the near bank, where Grandi and others had concealed themselves, waiting for the weak and exhausted animals to stagger by. They did not have to wait long. A mother and calf came over the embankment, but the female had dislocated her foreleg, probably when jumping into the water, and was limping badly

– a prime target. Two of the lionesses leaped from cover, brought her down and suffocated her in seconds. Another grabbed the calf, and it too was dead. Mbili and Tatu arrived to take over the adult beast, leaving the calf to the lionesses. All around them, wildebeest were on the move, heading away from the river and the prospect of fresh, short grass.

All it took was a few weeks of good hunting and once again all the members of the pride were looking plump and healthy. The young males showed signs of the mane they would grow in the not too distant future and, although some were still limping with the after-effects of malnutrition, most of the young females were ready to join in the hunt with their mothers and aunts. And in between the brief bouts of frantic activity, they were all able to relax in a way that only lions know how.

The pride ate well, but now that the migration was moving around their patch, it brought all manner of unwelcome guests. Nomads of either sex invaded and were chased off, but it also meant that Tatu could indulge his passion for illicit liaisons. He was absent for long periods yet again, leaving Mbili and the pride wide open to invasion and a possible takeover.

Three lions came over the rise. They were not from the neighbouring pride, but nomads. They started to roar. It was a warning to all-comers that they were a force to be reckoned with. Nobody messed with these boys. They walked confidently down the track and out across the plain. They plodded on, heads down like bloodhounds sniffing the ground. They had picked up the scent of something and they were tracking it carefully. The three stopped. The leading lion raised his head and grimaced. He had smelled something that interested him. They walked towards a scattering of rocks and boulders rocks interspersed with trees and bushes, moving slowly and carefully. They were certainly concerned about something.

Suddenly, a pair of lionesses emerged from the vegetation. The three males had been tracking them. It was Chipipi and Msichana and there was little they could do except flirt their way out of the predicament. Fortunately, there were no cubs with them and the rest of the pride was some distance away, but the presence of three mature lions in the Tingatinga Pride territory was a disturbing development and, as if to underline how vulnerable Mbili had become, there was another event that must have unnerved him.

Soon after the encounter with the three nomads, a mysterious lion turned up at a kill. Grandi had just brought down a gazelle and several of the Tingatinga females were bringing the surviving cubs to feed when the lone male stepped out from behind a thicket. The lionesses stopped immediately and glared, but the intruder, as bold as brass, walked up to the gazelle, grabbed it and took it for himself. One of the cubs, not realising the seriousness of the situation, ambled over to feed. The lion dropped the carcass, grabbed the cub and shook it violently. Grandi exploded, charging the male. He retreated. Two other females lunged forward, ready to bite him on the backside, but he leaped, swivelling almost 180 degrees in midair, and cuffed one of the females before trotting away. The badly injured cub was bleeding from its side and rear leg. It did not survive the night.

The following day, the mysterious lion appeared again. This time vultures dropping down to scavenge on the remains of a wildebeest had attracted the pride but, as they approached the carcass, out popped the lion again. He seized what was left. The lionesses were more wary this time. They sat down and watched his every move and, after ten minutes or so, he left the wildebeest and moved deliberately towards the females, his head held low. He did not look at them, but walked past and flopped on to the ground about 50 metres away. Ten minutes later he tried to approach, but the lionesses snarled and showed their teeth, and he drew back again.

They remained like this for the best part of an hour, by which time Mbili had arrived. Curiously, he ignored the intruder and lay down alongside the females. None of them moved until the stranger stood, accompanied by their hissings and snarls, and began sniffing the ground around them. Still Mbili did nothing. The lionesses began to feel uncomfortable with this male around and they got up and walked away. He then sniffed at the ground where they had lain. He was clearly looking for signs that any of them were receptive, and he was doing so in full view of Mbili.

Grandi kept an especially close eye on him, ready to pounce should she have to, but then Tatu arrived, returning from his most recent sojourn. At this, the stranger quickly got up and walked away, without looking back, and was not seen again . . . at least not alone again. Tatu watched him go, somewhat bemused, for Mbili had not lifted a paw against him.

Tatu, however, did not stay long. With no food on the table, he left, heading out towards the neighbour's territory. There he found the females he had been meeting surreptitiously, but none was in heat so he carried on, entering the territory of the northern neighbours. Again, he travelled undetected and chanced upon a nomadic female who had been following the herds during the migration but had been left behind. Tatu took the opportunity to introduce himself. She was not on heat, but soon would be. He hung around, waiting for the opportunity to mate. The female, in the meantime, set out to hunt. She searched for something relatively small that she could tackle alone, or something big that she could scavenge. Tatu went along with the expectation of scrounging a meal.

The lioness, however, was not a skilled hunter. She had had little success, barely getting by on meagre rations, but then she found a herd of cattle, guarded only by one small boy. They were irresistible. She stalked, pounced and killed one of the herd, an easy kill. The boy shouted in alarm, and it turned out that he was not alone after all. A band of 30 warriors armed with spears and knives suddenly appeared. The lioness left the dead steer and ran. By fleeing down a gully, out of sight of the war party, she escaped, but Tatu was trapped. He had been hiding in a thicket while the lioness was stalking and now the warriors surrounded him. Tatu tried to fight, but when the first spear hit him, he called out in excruciating pain. More spears pierced his body and he roared for the last time. The warrior who had thrown the first spear had the honour of cutting off his tail. He held it above his head and the others cheered. He had been a brave warrior that day and this was his badge of courage.

Things were little better back with the Tingatinga Pride. The three nomads had marched into its territory. They strutted with heads held high, their fine manes blowing in the wind. This time they meant business. They had tested the defences of the pride males and they were ready to take over.

Mbili saw them approaching. Grandi stood beside him, while the other females dropped back. Ndugu took the cubs and raced to the marsh. The nomads came closer, halted and roared. Mbili and Grandi roared back, but roaring was not going to settle this encounter. Mbili's lone male voice and Grandi's female roar was not going to impress these three. They were spoiling for a fight.

They came even closer. Mbili and Grandi stood their ground. The two sides traded roars, and then there was an eerie silence.

Nobody moved. One of the nomads scuffed his back feet on the ground, making everyone jump, but it ended the standoff. The three lions walked slowly forwards and stopped only a few metres from the two residents. One raised his head and grimaced, checking the air for the smell of the enemy. It was then that Mbili and Grandi realised who the mysterious stranger had been. They recognised him instantly. He was one of the three nomads, and he had been checking the resilience of the pride males and the reproductive state of the females – another Trojan horse. Previously, Tatu's timely appearance had put paid to any designs he might have had on the pride females and their territory, but now he was back and Tatu was dead. Mbili's prospects looked decidedly bleak.

One of the nomads suddenly lunged forward. It was one-on-one. Mbili gave as good as he got at first, but the nomad was a younger, fitter lion. They separated. Mbili had a gash across his face, a deep wound on his jaw, and his mane had large pieces missing. His opponent was hardly scratched. They launched at one another again, rising up on to their hind legs and crashing back down in a cloud of dust. They rolled, biting and scratching, whereupon one of the other nomads joined in the attack. Grandi immediately leaped on to him. She was more agile than he was, but he was altogether more powerful. She landed a blow to his face, but he came back with a barrage of lethal bites. The third nomad grabbed her from behind, bit into her back, breaking her spine in two places. She dropped to the ground, her body quivering. Then she lay still. Grandi was dead.

Her opponents turned on Mbili, so he fought with all three lions, but the outcome was inevitable. Eventually he rolled on to his back in submission. The nomads bit and scratched his rump, but they too had had enough. Mbili dragged himself to his feet and fled, with one of the nomads in a half-hearted pursuit. After a couple of kilometres, the nomad dropped back, leaving Mbili alone on the plains. The three new males had won the territory and the pride. The king had been deposed. He limped to the shade of an acacia tree and lay down on the ground.

It was not long before hyenas followed the trail of blood and were gathering around where Mbili lay. It was Kikuto, and she was ready to take the first bite. But Mbili was not finished yet. He got to his feet and lunged at her. Before she could jump back, he had grabbed her head in his still powerful jaws and crushed her skull as if it was paper. At last, he had revenged the death of his sister Moja. The other hyenas scattered. They would not be back that night. Mbili slept.

In the morning, the surviving Tingatinga Pride lionesses went to the marsh to collect their cubs. They called . . . once, twice, three times . . . but there was no answer, not even from Ndugu. The new males had killed them all. The mothers found the bodies amongst the reeds alongside the young lion. He might have been the weakest member of the pride but he must have put up an extraordinary fight. Ndugu and the cubs had paid the ultimate price. It was the inevitable outcome of a pride takeover. Now the new pride males would start afresh – it was the way of lions.

Several kilometres away, Mbili lay seriously injured. He rose with difficulty and began to limp across the dry grassland. His blond mane, once thick and shining, was matted with blood. Huge pieces were missing. His tail was bent and broken, and there were deep, red gashes down his flanks and rump. His lower jaw was hanging loose, probably broken, and several of his teeth were shattered. Clouds of flies were attracted by the congealing wounds, and crowded around his face. But he kept on walking, step after painful step, out of his former pride's territory, and right across the plains towards the highlands in the south.

After several days without eating, he was like a walking skeleton, little more than skin and bone. His mane had become ragged and his ribs could be seen clearly through his threadbare fur. Black areas on his face showed that he was losing hair from there as well. He moved stiffly, his scrawny muscles aching with every step.

He trekked for several more days and nights, hardly pausing to rest, and when he reached the steep slopes of the crater, he climbed until he reached the rim. Following the twists and turns of the elephant track, he dropped down through the forest and found the rocky slope where he was born. He lay down under a tree and tried to roar, but it was no more than a whimper. His life was slowly fading away. He licked his wounds one final time, and laid his head on the soft, green grass.

Not long after, a group of lions came by and one of their number walked over to where Mbili lay. It was an old lioness. She sniffed at the inert body and a hint of recognition appeared in her tired eyes. She stared, then turned. She walked slowly back to the others and they all continued on their way. The old lady hesitated, looked around one more time, and then followed the track to the crater floor. Mbili had come home and Masa was with her pride.

Acknowledgements and Resources

I would like to thank the many people who have contributed observations of African lions and other East African and southern African wildlife that have influenced events in this story, including Amanda Barrett, Peter Bassett, Brian Bertram, Lizzie Bewick, Stephen Bolwell, Adam Chapman, Malcolm Coe, Martin Colbeck, Dan Freeman, James Honeyborne, Colin Jackson, Simon King, Neil Lucas, Hugh Miles, Owen Newman, Craig Packer, Barry Paine, Dave Parkinson, Robin Pellew, Nigel Pope, Alan Root, Jonathan Scott, Warwick Sloss, Gavin Thurston, and the late Des Bartlett and Hugo von Lawick.

I also would like to single out my colleagues on the *Big Cat Diary* and *Big Cat Week* production teams based at the BBC's Natural History in Bristol, whose tales from Kenya's Masai Mara were the inspiration for *The Pride*. You can see their superbly crafted programmes on the following DVDs:

Big Cat Week: the complete first and second series BBC DVD 1921

Big Cat Week: the complete third series BBC DVD 2351

Big Cat Week: the complete fourth series BBC DVD 2831

If you would like to read more about lions and their natural history, you can do no better than dip into the books of *Big Cat Diary* presenter, wildlife photographer and author Jonathan Scott, who together with his wife Angela, have documented life on the East African plains:

Scott, Jonathan. *The Great Migration*, Elm Tree Books (London: 1988)

Scott, Jonathan. *Kingdom of Lions*, Kyle Cathie (London: 1992)

Scott, Jonathan and Angela Scott. *Big Cat Diary: Lion*, HarperCollins (London: 2002)

Collaboration between Scott and journalist and travel writer Brian Jackman resulted in two more engaging books on the Masai Mara:

Jackman, Brian and Jonathan Scott. *The Marsh Lions: The Story of an African Pride*, Elm Tree Books (London: 1982)

Jackman, Brian, and Jonathan Scott. *The Big Cat Diary: A Year in the Masai Mara*, BBC Books (London: 1994)

For a different perspective on lions, from prides in Botswana's Okavango Delta, take a look at the words and wonderful photographs of wildlife filmmakers Beverley and Dereck Joubert:

Joubert, Beverley and Dereck Joubert. *Relentless Enemies: Lions and Buffalo*, National Geographic (Washington DC: 2006)

More scholarly yet very accessible accounts of lion biology can be found in these books:

Bertram, Brian. *Pride of Lions*, J. M. Dent & Sons (London: 1978)

Guggisberg, C. A. W. *Simba: The Life of a Lion*, Bailey Bros. & Swinfen (London: 1961)

Guggisberg, C. A. W. *Wild Cats of the World*, David & Charles (Newton Abbot: 1975)

Kitchener, Andrew. *The Natural History of the Wild Cats*, Christopher Helm (London: 1991)

Schaller, George B. *The Serengeti Lion: A study of Predator-Prey Relations*, University of Chicago Press (Chicago: 1972)

Smuts, G. L. *Lion*, Macmillan (London: 1982)

To find out what it is like to be a research scientist in the Serengeti and Ngorongoro Crater, dip into the memoir from distinguished lion researcher Professor Craig Packer, from the University of Minnesota's Department of Ecology, Evolution and Behaviour:

Packer, Craig. *Into Africa* (with new postscript), The University of Chicago Press (Chicago: 1996)

If you would like to learn more about current research with lions, visit the website of the Lion Research Center:

http://www.lionresearch.org

And, if you are going on safari yourself, then be sure to have a copy of this book on hand: Estes, Richard Despard.

The Behaviour Guide to African Mammals, Russel Friedman Books (South Africa: 1971)

Scientific papers and articles referenced during research for *The Pride* include the following:

Bygott J. David, Brian C. R. Bertram, and Jeannette P. Hanby. 'Male lions in large coalitions gain reproductive advantages', *Nature* 282: 839–841 (1979)

Coulson, Tim. 'Population Ecology: Group Living and Hungry Lions', *Nature* 449: 996–997 (2007)

Fosbrooke, Henry. 'The stomoxys plague in Ngorongoro', *East African Wildlife Journal* 1: 124–126 (1963)

Frank, Laurence, and Craig Packer. 'Life Without Lions', *New Scientist* (25 October 2003)

Fryzell, John M., Anna Mosser, Anthony R. E. Sinclair, and Craig Packer. 'Group Formation Stabilizes Predator-Prey Dynamics', *Nature* 449: 1041–1043 (2007)

Gilbert, D. A., C. Packer, A. E. Pusey, J. C. Stephens, and S. J. O'Brien. 'Analytical DNA Fingerprinting in Lions: Parentage, Genetic Diversity, and Kinship', *The Journal of Heredity* 82(5): 378–386 (1991)

Grinnell, Jon, Craig Packer and Anne Pusey. 'Cooperation in male lions: kinship, reciprocity or mutualism?', *Animal Behaviour* 49: 95–105 (1995)

Grinnell, Jon, and Karen McComb. 'Maternal grouping as a defence against infanticide by males: evidence from field playback experiments on African lions', *Behavioural Ecology* 7 (1): 55–59 (1996)

Grinnell, Jon, and Karen McComb. 'Roaring and social communication in African lions: the limitations imposed by listeners', *Animal Behaviour* 62: 93–98 (2001)

Heinsohn, Robert and Craig Packer. 'Complex Cooperative Strategies in Group-Territorial African Lions', *Science* 269: 1260–1262 (1995)

Hopcraft, J. Grant C., Anthony. R. E. Sinclair, and Craig Packer. 'Planning for success: Serengeti lions seek prey accessibility rather than abundance', *Journal of Animal Ecology* 74: 559–566 (2005)

Kissui, Bernard M., and Craig Packer. 'Top-down population regulation of a top predator: lions in Ngorongoro Crater', *Proceedings of the Royal Society of London* (2004), published online and accessed on 25th September 2008 at: http://www. lionresearch.org/current_docs/m_pdf/regulation.pdf

McComb, Karen, Anne Pusey, Craig Packer, and Jon Grinnell. 'Female lions can identify potentially infanticidal males from their roars', *Proceedings of the Royal Society of London* 252: 59–64 (1993)

McComb K., C. Packer and A. E. Pusey. 'Roaring and numerical assessment in the contests between groups of female lions', *Animal Behaviour* 47:379–387 (1994)

Mills, Gus. 'About Lions: Ecology and Behaviour' (2007), from African Lion Working Group website, accessed on 6th October 2008 at: http://www.african-lion.org/lions.htm

Packer, Craig. 'Captives in the Wild', *National Geographic* 181: 122–136 (April 1992)

Packer, Craig. 'Coping with a Lion Killer', *Natural History* 6/96: 14–17 (1996)

Packer, Craig. 'Who Rules the Park?', *Wildlife Conservation,* June 1996, pp. 36–39 (1996)

Packer, Craig. 'Infanticide Is No Fallacy', *American Anthropologist* 102 (4): 829–857 (2001)

Packer, Craig, and Anne E. Pusey. 'Adaptations of Female Lions to Infanticide by Incoming Males', *The American Naturalist* 121: 716-728 (1983)

Packer, Craig, and Anne E. Pusey. 'Male Takeovers and Female Reproductive Parameters: A Simulation of Oestrus Synchrony in Lions', *Animal Behaviour* 31: 334–340 (1983)

Packer, Craig, and Anne E. Pusey. 'Infanticide in carnivores' in *Infanticide: Comparative and Evolutionary Perspectives*, edited by

Glen Hausfater and Sarah Blaffer Hrdy, Aldine (New York), pp. 31–42 (1984)

Packer, Craig, and Anne E. Pusey. 'Intrasexual Cooperation and the Sex Ration in African lions', *The American Naturalist* 130 (4): 636–642 (1987)

Packer, Craig, and Anne E. Pusey. 'Should a lion change its spots?', *Nature* 362: 595 (1993)

Packer, Craig, and Anne E. Pusey. 'Dispersal, Kinship, and Inbreeding in African Lions' in *The Natural History of Inbreeding and Outbreeding*, edited by N. W. Thornhill, University of Chicago Press (Chicago), pp. 375–391 (1993)

Packer, C., and A. E. Pusey. 'The Lack Clutch in a Communal Breeder: Lion Litter Size is a Mixed Evolutionarily Stable Strategy'. *The American Naturalist* 145 (5): 833–841 (1995)

Packer, Craig, and Anne E. Pusey. 'Divided We Fall: Cooperation among Lions', *Scientific American*, May 1997 pp. 32–39 (1997)

Packer, Craig, Anne E. Pusey, and Lynn E. Eberly. 'Egalitarianism in Female African Lions', *Science* 293: 690–693 (2001)

Packer C., D. Scheel and A. E. Pusey. 'Why lions form groups: food is not enough', *The American Naturalist* 136:1–19 (1990)

Packer C., D. A. Gilbert, A. E. Pusey, and S. J. O'Brien. 'A molecular genetic analysis of kinship and cooperation in African lions', *Nature* 351: 562–565 (1991)

Packer, Craig, Dennis Ikanda, Bernard M. Kissui, and Hadas Kushnir. 'Lion Attacks on Humans in Tanzania', *Nature* 436: 927–8 (2005)

Packer, Craig, and Lore Ruttan. 'The Evolution of Cooperative Hunting', *The American Naturalist* 132 (2): 159–198 (1988)

Packer, Craig, Marc Tatar, and Anthony Collins. 'Reproductive cessation in female mammals', *Nature* 392: 807–811 (1998)

Packer, Craig, Ray Hilborn, Anna Mosser, Bernard M. Kissui, Markus Borner, J. Grant C. Hopcraft, John Wilmshurst, Simon Mduma, Anthony R. E. Sinclair. 'Ecological Change, Group Territoriality, and Population Dynamics in Serengeti Lions', *Science* 407: 390–393 (2005)

Packer, Craig, Robert D. Holt, Peter J. Hudson, Kevin D. Lafferty, and Andrew P. Dobson. 'Keeping the herds healthy and alert: implications of predator control for infectious diseases', *Ecology Letters* 6: 797–802 (2003)

Packer, C., S. Altizer, M. Appel, E. Brown, J. Martenson, S. J. O'Brien, M. Roelke-Parker, R. Hofmann-Lehmann, and H. Lutz. 'Viruses of the Serengeti: patterns of infection and mortality in African lions', *Journal of Animal Ecology* 68: 1161–1178 (1999)

Packer, Craig, Susan Lewis and Anne Pusey. 'A comparative analysis of non-offspring nursing', *Animal Behaviour* 43: 265–281 (1992)

Pusey, Anne E., and Craig Packer. 'Non-offspring nursing in social carnivores: minimizing the costs', *Behavioural Ecology* 5 (4): 362–374 (1994)

Scheel D. 'Watching for lions in the grass: the usefulness of scanning and its effects during hunts *Animal Behaviour* 46: 695–704 (1993)

Scheel, D., and C. Packer. 'Group hunting behaviour of lions: a search for cooperation', *Animals Behaviour* 41: 697–709 (1991)

Troyer, Jennifer L., Jill Pecon-Slattery, Melody E. Roelke, Lori Black, Craig Packer, and Stephen J. O'Brien. 'Patterns of Feline Immunodeficiency Virus Multiple Infection and Genome Divergence in a Free-Ranging Population of African Lions', *Journal of Virology* 78 (7): 3777–3791 (2004)

Varty, John. 'Tiger Birth at Tiger Canyons', Newsletter 19 (2009), accessed on 7th April 2009 at: http://www.jvbigcats.co.za/newsletters19.htm

West, Peyton M, and Craig Packer. 'Sexual Selection, Temperature, and the Lion's Mane', *Science* 297: 1339–1343 (2002)

Whitman, Karyl, Anthony M. Starfield, Henley S. Quadling, and Craig Packer. 'Sustainable trophy hunting of African lions', published online (2004), Nature | doi: 10.1038/nature 02395 and accessed on 27th September 2008 at: http://www.nature.com/nature.